Praise for *Over 80*

Over 80 gives voice to those seldom heard in our culture: people 80 and older. Now in her ninth decade, Reynolds' witty and wise random reflections pour through her lens of longevity and a life well lived. Ageism, divorce, caregiving, the pandemic, the joys this former educator experienced converting haters of books into lifetime-readers, second chances, and more are shared from the perspective of someone whose longevity reminds her daily of her own mortality. Humor fills the book such as the author's vision of Mimi Avocada, the irreverent Goddess of the Universe, who appears to Reynolds during a church service. Living a long life, she writes, evolves from "first" experiences to one of "last" experiences. Reynolds has turned her longevity into a treasure trove of rich, touching insights and it is a gem worth reading repeatedly, and you will. Trust me, you will.

> —*Dev Berger, retired health policy consultant, aging advocate and writer*

Wisdom suggests that as we grow older, we hold onto our attitudes, beliefs, and other lifelong characteristics. Marilyn Reynolds, at 86 years-old, admits slowing down and memory loss, but in defying wisdom, she has found gratifying new interests. *Over 80* offers humor and poignancy, a wealth of 'let's share' even the less welcome changes, suggesting a trouble shared is almost a trouble halved.

> -- San Francisco Book Review

Reading Marilyn Reynolds's *Over 80* is like having a conversation with a close friend. Neither depressing or sugar-coated, Reynolds' anecdotes and insights are a bit like answers to the questions many of us in retrospect wish we had asked our mothers and grandmothers. Her narrative voice is friendly, interesting, and honest. I highly recommend her book and warn you that you may be motivated to begin writing your own reflections.

> —*Ruth Saxton, author of* The Book of Old Ladies

While there's no universally accepted description of healthy aging, Marilyn Reynolds provides a humorous, relatable, and refreshingly honest perspective on a topic that can be as hard to face as it is inevitable. Her self-deprecating wit make concerns about aging that are daily brought up in my office approachable and provide an inspiring example of navigating unavoidable challenges with both pragmatism and hope. While I can't completely support her red meat, martinis, and wine diet, she makes a strong case that a lifetime of curiosity crossed with a touch of skepticism and an underlying resilience can carry you a long way. Her journey provides countless insights and a thoughtful perspective that would benefit all my aging patients. You won't regret joining her for this ride.

—*Katerina Christiansen, MD*

Through humor, acceptance and wisdom, Reynolds shares stories and insights about "...the unknown territory of aging..." as she shares reflections on being in her ninth decade of life. This book is about finding meaning in daily life at any age, and most poignantly, Reynolds shares what has fed her soul from her many years of being an educator. Dealing with unknown challenges and loss, she takes us on a journey as she names the necessities of life, explores healthy aging to the richness of memories and what makes life worth living. It is full of life lessons.

—*Cynthia Davis, gerontologist and hospice chaplain*

OVER 80

REFLECTIONS ON AGING

Marilyn Reynolds

New Wind Publishing
Sacramento, California

New Wind Publishing
Copyright © 2022 by Marilyn Reynolds.

Portions of this book have appeared, in slightly different form, in the following publications: *Los Angeles Times; Love Lifespan, Volume 4; Over 70 And I Don't Mean MPH; Soul of the Narrator, Volume 8.*

This is a work of nonfiction that reflects the author's present recollections of experiences. Some names have been changed.

Library of Congress Control Number: 2022909833

ISBN 978-1-929777-29-7 (paperback)
ISBN 978-1-929777-30-3 (ebook)
1. Reynolds, Marilyn—1935. 2. Authors, American—20th century—Memoir. 3. Aging. 4. Humor. 5. Essays. I. Title.

Cover design and collage by Karen Phillips
Marilyn Reynolds photo by Amy Shamberg-Pero

Over 80: Reflections on Aging / Marilyn Reynolds. -- 1st ed.

New Wind Publishing
Sacramento, California 95819
www.newwindpublishing.com

"The best I can do is offer a firsthand account of a small life with a very limited point of view."
~Garrison Keillor

TABLE OF CONTENTS

Who You'll Meet in These Pages

Sharon (daughter), Doug (My Favorite Son-in-Law), Subei and Lena (granddaughters)

Cindi (daughter),

Matt (son)

Dale (brother), Marg (sister-in-law), Corry (niece)

Roger (UUSS Minister and dog-sharing partner)

Anara (friend, neighbor, fellow traveler)

Dear Reader

This is a collection of reflections and random thoughts dealing with various aspects and experiences of life in my ninth decade. I now fall into the "old-old category," a stage of life we don't often see reflected back to us in books or other media. I hope Over 80 is at least a small counter balance.

When I first started this project near my eightieth birthday, I was thinking that my 80s would probably not be much different than my 70s. But they are. Although I continue to be in good health it's obvious my body is farther along into the decaying process. I'm slower in speech and getting in and out of a car. In some public situations I'm less visible. Although I pass the basic cognitive function test with flying colors, I definitely don't remember names or other specific details as I once did. So, not exactly like the 70s.

On my first read through, I saw that I had included nothing about books and reading—so crucial throughout my life and even more so in my 80s. There was also nothing about life-giving laughter. That I rectified, as you can read in "The Gift of Reading, Parts 1 and 2: The Little Free Library," and in "The Secret to Longevity?"

In the process of assembling all these essays, I became aware of other important aspects of my 80s life that had been given short shrift. The subjects range from light-hearted, even silly, to darker aspects of loss and impending death, but music was missing; how did that happen? Music is, at various times, a comfort, an energizing force, a door to the past, or a quick kick of grief. Not a day passes without a musical offering. "Standing on the Promises" transports me back to the age of four or five, sitting on the bathroom counter, watching my father shave, my own face lathered with Yardley's shaving cream, my father humming in his soft tenor voice, adding the words once both of our faces were cleaned with the hot wet towel, then patted dry: "Standing on the promises of Christ, my king . . ."

With "Ode to Joy" from Beethoven's Ninth, I'm walking down the aisle to meet the one with whom I'll share the next thirty-eight years. With Burl Ives and "The Little White Duck," women now in their sixties are girls again, singing along. A Chopin waltz brings to mind Arthur Rubinstein at the Dorothy Chandler Pavilion, rising from the piano bench to drive a phrase home. "Brother Can You Spare a Dime?" brings back the loss of Mike in unexpected ways, and "Mad Dogs and Englishmen" has me laughing again at the perfect comic timing of his remembered antics. How could I not have included the necessities of music in my reflections?

And I see that I've written very little about the strong love and connection with family. My grown-up kids, Sharon, Cindi, and Matt, and my brother, Dale, each deserve at least 800 words; at least as many words as, say, trying to remember the name of one of the Dirty Dozen Pinochle players. And what kind of grandmother am I anyway, that none of the grandkids gets more than a sentence or two? And what about the lifelong friends without whom times in my life would have been dull and gray? More thorough reflections on music? Family? Friends? Too late. Maybe next time.

With love,
Marilyn

Becoming 80

I sit at my desk, sorting through a shoebox full of random photos, looking for some image that might be an embarrassment to my son-in-law Doug at his upcoming 65th birthday celebration. In truth, MFSIL (My Favorite Son-In-Law) doesn't embarrass easily. Probably an amusing picture will do. He *is* easily amused.

Shuffling through a handful of photos, the one that jumps out at me is not of Doug, but of me on my 80th birthday, September 13, 2015. I am sitting at the head of a large table in the dining room of the Noepe Center for the Arts in Martha's Vineyard. Seated around the table are nine other writing workshop participants.

Crystal glasses with varying levels of wine, dessert plates with leftover crumbs of the beautiful (tasteless) birthday cake from the local gluten free bakery. Candles light the room. Everyone in the picture is smiling broadly.

I'm wearing a grey top and, although it isn't shown in the picture, I remember a matching grey skirt. Close-cropped curly grey hair, silver earrings. Around my neck is a gauzy white scarf with subtle pastel stripes. I often wear scarves these days, partly because my neck goes stiff and cold in even the faintest of drafts, and partly because my once Audrey Hepburn-esque neck has turned into my granny's neck, complete with loose skin and wattles.

Except for one person at the table, a Sacramento poet I've traveled here with, I've not seen any of these people since the photo was taken five years ago, yet I still remember each of them and their work. Whether fiction or non-fiction, fantasy, poetry or memoir, writers bare their souls. We have nothing to offer except what is within us. Even a story about a dragon family living in a space satellite in some alternate universe still comes from its author's own insights, observations, and experiences. After two weeks of sharing our writing, we got to know each other's unforgettable souls. We all became memorable to one another.

The picture shows me with a full, relaxed smile; glowing, if an 80-year-old woman can ever be described as glowing. At this, the beginning of my ninth decade, my heart is lightened, my spirit unburdened.

When my husband Mike was diagnosed with Frontotemporal Dementia in 2009, I struggled to educate myself. This was a particular form of dementia I'd never heard of until the neurologist's diagnosis. Beyond whatever medical information was available, I searched in vain for anything from an ordinary caregiver's point of view. I desperately wanted to know how others were coping in that role, where they found support, how they were managing their everyday lives. Such information was not to be had. It was after that futile search that I promised myself I would write the story I wished I could have read when Mike was first diagnosed—the story of an everyday caregiver's experience, something with which I might have connected, a story that would have helped me feel less alone.

As the author of thirteen books—eleven for teens, one for teachers, and a collection of essays, I knew how to write a book. But a book about taking care of my FTD-afflicted husband? Revisit some of the saddest, most heart wrenching and painful experiences of my whole life for the sake of getting it on paper? But a promise is a promise and I embarked on the project shortly after Mike was moved to a secure facility in early 2011. I started writing a straight, chronological story. It was a lot to relive, though. I tried writing it in third person, then experimented with it as a piece of fiction, or a potential novel. I even wrote four chapters from our *dog's* point of view! But those choices, though easier to write, seemed somehow dishonest. Finally, I wrote in my own voice a mostly chronological record, interspersed with short accounts of our pre-FTD lives.

In the past it had generally taken me about nine months to write a book, nine months from conception to delivery. That was not to be the case with this one. Even though Mike was no longer at home with me, my time was filled with

Mike-related tasks—finding a new place for him after his angry outbursts got him evicted from the first place, manipulating the very difficult financial situation that came with needing to spend $3,800 a month for his care. There were numerous appointments with doctors and dentists, conferences with care home administrators, plus regular visits with Mike. None of this was conducive to writing a book, but I managed to keep my creative juices flowing by regular meetings with a local writing group, and for three summers in a row I attended the writing retreat at the Noepe Center where I completed chunks of the caregiving chronicle.

When the birthday photo was taken, I'd just finished a final draft of that story; it was ready to go to the publisher. The promise I made to myself was finally fulfilled. That heavy burden was lifted. No wonder the picture shows a glowing eighty-year-old!

Although in truth Mike's life was taken from him years before he actually stopped breathing, at the time this picture was taken, he'd been dead for nine months. With his death my life had been returned to me. Although that may sound harsh, it's the simple truth, which I prefer to flowery euphemisms.

'Til Death or Dementia Do Us Part was published in 2017. Even though it is a memoir, not a self-help book, I occasionally get an email or a rare letter by post, saying the book has helped a

reader feel less alone, and I'm reassured that my long ago promise was one worth keeping.

Now, with my 86th birthday fast approaching, I'm more aware than ever that the time I have left in this aging body, on this endangered earth, in this threatened democracy, is quickly diminishing. I want to use the time well, to find joy and meaning in each day, to live with purpose.

Unlike the sad and arduous writing required for *'Til Death or Dementia Do Us Part*, I approached this writing with a lighter heart, as if writing a long letter to a contemporary friend, a soul mate. With *Over 80 . . .* my overriding purpose has been to give voice to the elders whose voices are too seldom heard. That's the longer term goal. My immediate purpose is to find some embarrassing, or at least an amusing, picture of MFSIL to unveil at his 65th birthday celebration. There's got to be *something* in this overstuffed shoebox.

Secrets to Longevity?

On my most recent birthday—the 86th—Roger, one of the ministers at the Unitarian Universalist Society of Sacramento and my dog-sharing partner, asked, "What's your secret to longevity?"

"Plenty of red meat, martinis, and wine, and not too much exercise."

"I'll pray for you," he said.

Word of my secret to longevity got out and a friend stopped by on my birthday with a nicely wrapped package containing a bottle of vodka, a bottle of Cabernet, and a beautiful hunk of raw steak from Whole Foods. I had steak and Cabernet for dinner the next night—delicious! The vodka I saved for a later martini time.

Of course, my answer to Roger was flip; my food and liquid consumption is broader than indicated. Still, I do eat more red meat than is recommended and my weekly consumption of wine also exceeds recommendations. My occasional one martini is within reasonable health guidelines, though following it with wine at dinner is probably not.

I eat an abundance of cheese, douse my coffee with heavy cream, and slather butter on my morning muffin. My good cholesterol is high and the bad stuff is low. A recent angiogram showed no gummed-up arteries.

On Tuesdays, I get a fairly good workout in an hour-long Silver Sneakers group; sometimes I add an online workout later in the week. Even though I go for walks in the neighborhood my weekly step count is embarrassingly low. So clearly my level of physical activity is far below accepted recommendations.

Well . . . what *is* my secret to longevity? It's all just a crap shoot, isn't it? Maybe I have a longevity gene. My mother's side was long-lived, though they were also prone to dementia in their later years. That's nothing I aspire to. My father died at fifty-eight but he probably would have lived much longer had he not been a daily heavy drinker. Most of his ten brothers and sisters lived into their eighties.

Maybe it's attitude? In spite of the state of the world, I lean toward contentment. And I have the capacity to laugh at life's foibles and ironies, YouTube videos of puppies, and my own shortcomings. Laughter may be the true key to my longevity. At least it makes a long life worth living.

Being voted the wittiest girl in the 10th grade was my major achievement in high school. Neither I (nor the wittiest boy) got very good grades. Joining in the hearty laughter elicited from one's friends by some smart-ass remark of mine may have damned my academic success, but it's well worth having if it leads to healthful longevity.

In the over-100 crowd, there are a variety of active models to choose from. There's the 105-year-old New Jersey resident who starts every day with a serving of nine gin-soaked golden raisins; another 105-year-old who has whiskey in his tea every morning and two shots of scotch in a glass of lemonade every night; a 117-year-old French nun whose secret is red wine; a San Francisco centenarian woman who exercises every day but has a regular bedtime snack of one beer and three potato chips, and yet another one who attributes her longevity to regular Big Macs.

Wherever the gift of longevity comes from, I'm happy it's found me, and I want to use it well, meeting the challenges that come with being an "old-old," and enjoying the simple gifts of the remaining days.

Realities of Life in the 80s— Part 1: The Four Pillars

At this stage of life, with the responsibilities of full-time teaching long behind me, I have the luxury of time to reflect, write, read, be with friends and family. I no longer struggle for self-improvement, no longer care that I'm ten pounds overweight. Like my old role model, Popeye the Sailor Man, I accept that I yam what I yam.

The Internet offers an abundance of advice on healthy aging, some detailed and complex, some simple and straightforward. The Ten Steps to Healthy Aging made sense to me when I read them a while back, but then I could never remember what they were! The Mayo Clinic describes the Four Pillars of Healthy Aging as Nutrition, Exercise, Connection, and Purpose. These at least offer guidelines that I can hold in my now sieve-like brain as I travel the road to decrepitude.

I live in a neighborhood that offers ample opportunities for safe, pleasant walking. I belong to a gym and even, sometimes, go there. Between Raley's Market and Whole Foods, Selland's Market-Cafe, and In-N-Out Burger, I have access to plenty of food choices. (Oops! I just read that In-N-Out offers significant support to the Republican Party. Even though my mouth waters whenever I get within 500 feet of one of their drive-thrus, I now find it necessary to boycott In-N-Out.)

As for connection, I'm fortunate to have close ties to my extended family, and to have a number of close friendships. There are still people in my life who I love, still people who love me. Such bonds are crucial to my well-being. I am also grateful for my connection with the Unitarian Universalist Society of Sacramento. It is reassuring to know that I'm part of a congregation that works for the good of others. The sermons and reflections of Sunday services help me maintain a perspective on my life in relation to the broader world.

There's also a sense of connection that reaches beyond my physical environment—a sense that although I'm smaller than a speck of dust in this vast universe, I am nevertheless a part of it all. At this age, like every cognizant age-mate, I am aware of my own imminent mortality—an awareness that was less conscious in me earlier on. I like life and hope that I've got several good years left, but whether it's years, or months, or days, I trust that the universe is well-ordered and benign, and that whatever does or does not come after this life is nothing to fear. I find a sense of purpose through social connections and family, through writing endeavors, and most recently, through the Little Free Library project. (More about that in "The Gift of Reading, Part 2: The Little Free Library.")

The Four Pillars don't cover some of the less concrete aspects of being over eighty, aspects I don't want to ignore. For one thing, there's the task of facing one's own mortality—a big issue for my demographic. At least it's a big issue for all who are grounded in reality. There's the need to take care of the business side of death so our families won't have to. We need to be sure that our wills are up to date. Get our financial records in order. If we want a service or celebration of our lives, offer guidance for those who will be charged with that task. And where will Great-Gramma's china and silver, and other treasured items go? And . . . what will become of my own unique, treasured self?

Recognizing that our end is near leads many of us to the task of evaluating our lives. Did we do right by our children? Our spouses? Our work? Ourselves? What has it all meant?

What about loss? Nothing in the Four Pillars confronts the reality that life in one's 80s is one loss after another, after another. We lose partners and close friends, memory and mobility. The Four Pillars don't address the necessities of laughter and joy, music and books. If I didn't have these in my life, I'm sure I'd be dead by now, or at least I'd want to be.

So, facing death. Assessing life. Accumulated loss with more to come. Spirituality. The joys that make life worth living. I'm reassured to see there's some of all that scattered throughout this collection, reassured that the Four Pillars offers me a jumping-off place, not a set of boundaries.

Realities of Life in the 80s— Part 2: The Markers

It seems strange to me that I'm suddenly so damned old. Oh, I know. It didn't happen *suddenly*. It took me eighty-six years to get here. It feels sudden, though, and the linear second by second, minute by minute, hour by hour, day by day, year by year time measurement reflects a calendar reality but denies my own personal perception of my age. It's a common theme with friends who are approaching, or are already into their eighties: a cognitive dissonance. Our inner sense of ourselves is younger, maybe somewhere around fifty, but then we get a glimpse in the mirror, or there's a sciatica flare-up, or our diminished night vision prohibits driving after dark, and reality intrudes on our younger self-image.

I'm one of the lucky ones, healthy, active, socially engaged. Except for needing help with the occasional house repair, heavy lifting, or tech support, I'm fully able to care for myself. Younger friends claim me as some sort of role model for aging. I don't identify with the common perception of people in my age group. And yet as the mirror is a reality check, so is the "Aging: What to Expect" information on the Mayo Clinic website. Here's how I fare:

Bone and joint changes—I'm not stooped and according to bone density evaluations am not afflicted with osteoporosis. But, uh oh. Somewhere along the way I've lost an inch in height.

Chronic diseases—Well, there is high blood pressure, controlled by meds, but I suppose it still counts. Hmmm. And there's the pacemaker.

Chronic mucus hypersecretion—Nope. What the hell is *that* anyway?

Dental problems—So okay. I'm scheduled to have a broken tooth extracted next week.

Digestive problems—Nope.

Essential tremor—Nope.

Eyesight—Yep. Cataract surgery coming up.

Falls—Nope.

Gait change—Maybe a little.

Hair becomes grayer and thinner—Well duh!

Diminished hearing—Yep.

Heart becomes less efficient in old age—Yep, but thank you pacemaker.

Immune function becomes less efficient in old age—Doesn't seem to be the case.

Lungs provide less oxygen—Nope.

Mobility impairment—Nope.

Pain, rheumatological or malignant—Nope.

Sexuality, adapting sexual activity to accommodate physical, health, and other changes may be challenging—How the hell would I know?? Untested over the past decade.

Skin loses elasticity, becomes drier, more lined and wrinkled—Yep.

Wounds and injuries take longer to heal, more likely to leave permanent scars—Yep.

Sleep trouble—Sometimes.

Taste buds diminish—Yep.

Thirst perception decreases—Maybe.

Urinary incontinence—Nope.

Voice weakens and becomes breathy—Nope.

~

That's eleven yeses and three maybes out of the 24 physical markers of old age. Plus my hands and feet sometimes go numb. I'm afraid I have to own up to being physically old.

Then there are the mental markers:

Dependence may bring feelings of incompetence and worthlessness—Nope.

Caution and antipathy toward risk-taking—Some.

Depressed mood—Occasionally.

Greater fearfulness regarding finances, crime, loss of health, reduced mental and cognitive ability, possible dementia—Some but, you know, accept what I can't change, change what I can.

Set in one's ways or stubbornness—My family might say that's the case but more an aspect of my personality than a result of old age.

To recap, I don't feel worthless, though a sense of incompetence is not foreign to me. I'm not any more fearful than I've ever been, but I've become much more cautious than I once was. My short-term memory has gone missing and it can take anywhere from two to three hours to never for me to remember a specific detail of my life, say, the name of the Berkeley theatre that Mike and I once had season tickets to, or that one restaurant that has such good Thai food. So I guess I have to own up to being mentally old, too.

Wherever I now land on the scales of physical and mental markers for old age, I can be certain that I'll need to say yes to more and more of them in the near future. Either that, or I'll be dead. Neither prospect is appealing. The immediate future though, say, the next week, *is* appealing—an exercise class, dinner with a longtime friend, books to read, my turn with Lily, good walking weather . . . best to focus on the short term.

My So-Called Spiritual Journey—Part 1

With longevity's gift of perspective, leisure time for reflection, and the awareness that my days are numbered, I find myself revisiting experiences that built the foundation for what might loosely be described as my spiritual journey, contemplating long-held beliefs and disbeliefs, deciding what to keep and what to throw away.

From the childhood certainty of a heaven where people who believed in Jesus go to live for all eternity after their earthly deaths, to the acceptance of dust to dust realism, I've long grappled with the big questions.

Because of my early Sunday School experiences, Jesus and his dad played a significant part in my own youthful search for answers to questions of creation and eternity. The very first dream I can remember was from a time when I was probably four years old or younger, because I hadn't yet learned to swing by pumping my legs. In the dream, I am small and lonely, sitting in one of four swings in a playground. I'm gripping the chains that attach to the sturdy supporting metal frame. The seats are made of a rubber-like material that curves upward at each side of my light body. There is sand underneath my dangling feet.

The children in the other three swings each have a grown-up standing behind them, pushing, laughing, offering encouraging words.

I sit in my becalmed swing, watching the others riding up and down, up and down, and I'm fervently wishing for someone to come push me. Just give me one little push! I'm only wishing, not even praying, when a man comes walking toward me. He is surrounded by a soft, glowing light and he's wearing a long white dress. He smiles at me and I smile back. I think he is Jesus, the one from the Sunday School picture who talks sort of funny, saying stuff like "Suffer the little children to come unto me." I feel safe. I already like Jesus because of that song about how he loves me, and also because he's a friend of my Granny's.

He doesn't speak. He just walks around behind me and gives me a push. His hands against my back are so gentle I hardly feel them, but the push is so strong it sends me soaring. I fly higher than I've ever been, back and forth, back and forth, never losing height or momentum. It's thrilling but not scary and I know it can go on and on and on.

I don't remember how the dream ended. Maybe it just drifted away with the rhythmic movement of the swing. What I do remember is that the very next Sunday I rushed into my classroom to look carefully at the picture of Jesus. He was definitely the one who had given me a push.

That Sunday I sang "Jesus Loves Me" with great fervor and enthusiasm.

The first hairline crack in the foundation of my faith came when I was probably around six. The boy across the street told me there was no such thing as Santa Claus and only babies believed there was. My mother assured me there was definitely a Santa Claus and I couldn't trust everything Richard Metz said. But I'd been put on alert and it took no time at all to realize that the Santa stories were lies and that Richard Metz was more trustworthy than my own mother.

Once I'd learned the truth about Santa, I developed nagging doubts about God and Jesus, who both fell into the same too-good-to-be-true category as the magical man with the flying reindeer. But the adults around me seemed to take God and Jesus a little more seriously than they did Santa, and I wanted to believe, so I continued to say my prayers and to think God might be listening.

The next fissure in my faith foundation came when I was around eight years old and Granny took me to Angelus Temple, the church of the famed Aimee Semple McPherson. I often spent Saturday night with my grandmother in her trailer down on Garvey Boulevard in South San Gabriel. Sunday mornings we would ride a city bus to the corner of Hollywood and Vine. From there we would walk a few blocks to The Little Country Church of Hollywood where we would hear the Goose Creek Quartet sing about Jesus, and Sister Sarah would read letters that testified to the joys of salvation after lives of horrible sins. The preacher's name was Fagin (I don't think I'm making this up!) and he delivered his Bible-wielding, fire-and-brimstone sermons with great passion. I was captivated by the watery spray that punctuated his pleas for surrender and his promises of salvation. Decades later, when a professor of linguistics referred to "plosive consonants," Dr. Fagin's spray leapt to memory.

Although Dr. Fagin sometimes spoke for so long that my butt hurt, I sat quietly without squirming because if I was a good girl (and I always was) Granny would take me to the Pig-n-Whistle for lunch. The menus there doubled as masks of cute pig faces and I could always make Granny laugh by donning the mask and oinking. It was many years before I recognized the irony of the adorable pig faces on one side of the menu and the link sausages on the other.

Why Granny had chosen Angelus Temple rather than The Little Country Church of Hollywood on that particular day is now lost to me. It may have been that some well-known missionary was speaking. If I've got the timing right, the year was 1943. Sister Aimee was probably there in her flowing white gown but, as memorable as she's reputed to be, I have no recollection of her that day. What I do remember is the spectacular testimony of the featured missionary's salvation.

He began by speaking of his mission's work with heathen sun god worshipers in darkest Africa. There was a wobbly movie of near-naked Black men dancing in a jungle clearing in frantic homage to the brightly shining sun. Then the same men were shown clothed and subdued in prayer before a large white cross in a wood-frame church.

Here's the part that really got me, though. In a dramatic accounting, punctuated by light and sound effects, the missionary told of how he had been a terrible sinner, living in thrall to the devil, speeding toward an eternity in the fires of hell. God kept calling to him but he wouldn't listen. He was an atheist!

As the missionary spoke of that night when God had been particularly insistent, he walked from the podium to center stage and entered a previously unlit set—a replica of the kitchen where he had once lived. On the table was an ashtray overflowing with spent cigarette butts, opened and apparently empty cans of pork and beans, and a nearly empty bottle of whiskey. The convincingly realistic sink and counter along the back wall of the set were filled with dirty dishes. In sharp contrast to the Godless filth of the kitchen were pretty gingham curtains that decorated the window above the sink—the only remaining evidence of the loving wife who'd been driven away by her husband's sinful ways.

Leaning against the table in the midst of his own squalor, the missionary told of his decision to put an absolute end to whatever crazy notion of God had been hounding him. Gathering himself to his full height, he gave the air above him a violent punch upward as he cried out, "God, if there be a God, let him show Himself unto me!" He stood for a moment in the silence. Then, both fists lifted toward the heaven he denied, his voice amplified by unseen microphones, he cried out again, "God, if there be a God, let him show Himself unto me!" Again . . . silence.

But at his third, ear-shattering demand, "God, if there be a God, let him show Himself unto me!" a sustained roar of thunder rocked the very space around us. A blindingly bright ball of light shot through the window, shattering the glass and surrounding the doubting sinner as he dropped to his knees in terror. The voice of God, deep and resonant, answered. "Here am I. Walk in my light!"

Although the cliché had not yet entered our daily speech, it is safe to say of the missionary's experience, "The rest is history."

At home the next evening, I could barely wait for my mother to leave to pick my father up at his market. I'd been waiting all day for the time I'd have the house to myself. "Don't you want to go with me to get Daddy?" she asked.

I shook my head no, not meeting her eyes. Usually I'd have gone with her. I liked to be in the market after closing time, to help scrape the blocks clean and get a quick snack of sliced cheese or a bite of raw hamburger. But I had other things on my mind right then.

"Well . . . I won't be long," she said. "If anyone rings the doorbell, don't answer it."

As soon as I heard the car leave the driveway, I went to the kitchen and raised my fists heaven-ward. I hoped my mother wouldn't be angry about the shattered window. "God, if there be a God, let him show Himself unto me!" I called out with all my might. Brownie came running in from his warm spot by the fireplace in the living room and stood in front of me, ears perked forward in a way that implied a question.

I stretched even taller, took a deep breath, waved my fists even more forcefully and shouted, "God, if there be a God, let him show Himself unto me!"

Brownie barked and jumped at me, wagging his tail, then crouching in his "let's play" posture.

For my third plea to God I stood on the kitchen chair, reached even closer to the ceiling and bellowed out, "God, if there be a God, let him show Himself unto me!"

Brownie's barks matched the volume of my pleas and we went on like this, Brownie barking and me shouting to God until the headlights of the Pontiac flashed across the window. I jumped down from the chair and slid it back where it be-longed. By the time my parents walked through the door, Brownie and I were stretched out in front of the fireplace in a tranquil domestic scene, me with a book propped on my chest and Brownie with his nose resting against my leg. I pretended to be engrossed in the book, but really, I was contemplating the lack of evidence for God in my life. If God had come to the sinning missionary but not to me, what good was He anyway?

The seed of cynicism grew and, although I continued to attend church with my grandmother and sometimes Sunday School at a church near my home, I couldn't give my heart totally to God as I was supposed to do because He had not appeared to me that Monday evening when I tried with such eager anticipation to summon Him.

Now though, having revisited that long ago time of my life, I wonder, did I miss something that evening? I cried out to God and Brownie came running, and with each shouted plea, Brownie tried harder and harder to gain my attention. And I'm thinking, maybe my young mind didn't totally understand the GOD/DOG/GOD reality, and God really had come to me, standing before me, wagging His tail and barking His head off.

~

I never did experience the sought after bolt-of-lightning message from God that would eliminate all doubts, but I later had something akin to a religious experience when Mimi Avocada, the Grand Goddess of the Harmonic Universe, revealed herself to me. Did I make this up? I don't know. It seems as if it happened.

It is the Christmas season, 1992. Hollywood Presbyterian Church. I am sandwiched between my eighty-one-year-old mother, Esther, and her seventy-year-old sister, Hazel, in a pew near the front. This church, where Mike is the tenor soloist, is a place my mother and aunt love, and I can barely tolerate. The last time I was here, over a year ago, I went in feeling fine and returned home with such a severely stiff neck that I couldn't turn my head more than half an inch in either direction. It was an extremely painful condition and it lasted long enough for my chiropractor to buy a new car. I interpreted that as a divine message telling me to stay away from the Presbyterians, at least in a church setting, but there are times, such as this one, when it seems best to be here.

Mike smiles down at me from his place in the choir. I smile back, glad that even after twenty-five years of marriage his smile still brings me pleasure. Mike is one of four paid soloists at this church and, except for several weeks in the summer, he is here every Thursday night for choir practice and every Sunday morning for two services. It worries me that some of the pap and drivel he hears from the pulpit might seep in, even though I know that his experience is in the music and not the words, and that he seldom listens to the sermon anyway. And, as the choir rises and fills the building with "And the Glory of the

Lord" from Handel's Messiah, I am reminded that the music here is definitely not pap and drivel.

I admit that the church itself looks inviting: hundreds of huge, bright red poinsettias decorate the chancel steps. The dark wooden pews are deeply burnished from decades of polishing and waxing. Plush royal blue cushions pad the seats and plush royal blue carpeting pads the aisles. It is carefully maintained, a beautiful structure, built to the glory of God, but "no one comes to the father except through the son" is, to me, ridiculous. Nevertheless, here I sit.

I am here this evening because my mother wants to hear Christmas music. Because she wants to hear Mike sing. Because I know it is important for her to get out and do some of the things she has always done. I'm also here because of guilt and obligation, and, let's hope, at least a little bit of love.

A "silent" stroke, drink, age, have all taken their toll on my mother. She has called me several times a day for the past week to remind me that I promised to bring her to this service. Now she is fidgeting.

"Praise God from whom all blessings flow. Praise Her all creatures here below. Praise Her above the heavenly hostess. Praise mother, daughter and holy ghost-ess."

I sing with conviction, though I am definitely not a singer. Mike's voice, when he decides to use it freely, soars, reaching the highest rafters and the deepest soul. My singing voice is cramped, limited to a range of about five notes, so I can safely shift hymn lyrics to fit my own theological standards without the risk of offending any of the believers around me. I don't want to be offensive; I only want to follow the dictates of "to thine own self be true."

The perpetually-tanned reverend-doctor-minister stands before us, arms outstretched, wearing a full flowing, custom tailored, royal blue robe. His theatrically honeyed voice speaks of the babe in the manger—the Christ child. The Christina child, I think, continuing to amuse myself by changing holy genders.

My mother tells me, loudly, that she has to go to the bathroom.

"This should be over in about twenty minutes," I whisper.

"I don't know if I can wait that long," she says.

The woman in front of us turns and throws a frown our way.

"Shall I take you right now?" I ask, again whispering, hoping my mother will take her cue from me and answer back softly.

"No. Pretty soon, though," she says, full voice, checking her watch as if it means something to her.

I look at the exit sign, calculating the least disturbing way to get my mother from where we are to where she wants to be. It looks different than it did just moments ago. Not only are the letters brighter, the whole sign is bathed in light. It reminds me of the old paintings where Jesus is encompassed in a luminous aura. I feel drawn toward the expanding glow that now floats over the door. At the same time, I am inescapably anchored to my mother. Yearning toward a glowing exit sign is new to me. Feeling trapped by my mother's neediness is not.

A roar fills my head, like the roar of an angry sea, or of five o'clock freeway traffic. I close my eyes and listen to inside me—to the roar of *why*. Why couldn't my mother and I have been soul mates? We are each, in our own way, decent people. If we could ever have gone beyond superficialities, wouldn't it be easier to be patient with her now, in her failing years?

A dizzying turbulence of whispering, whirling noises fills my being and then—another sound, starting low, a growing hum of human voices, instruments, harmonies along a scale of a thousand octaves. I am floating on consonance, elevated a plane above the minister, the choir, my mother, the plush royal blues of carpets and cushions.

"Marilyn," a voice echoes in pure tones.

I nod, keeping my eyes closed, straining to focus on the welling within me.

"Daughter." The voice is rich and resonant, beyond operatic, speaking in chords.

"What??" I whisper, opening my eyes for an instant, seeing as if from a distance the elderly woman who is still checking her watch.

"She, Esther, is your carnal mother. I am your soul mother."

Reaching inward for an image to accompany the voice, I catch glimpses of deep purples and reds, flowing silk against an indigo blue.

"Who are you?"

"I am your soul mother, the Grand Goddess of the Harmonic Universe."

I look around, wondering if anyone else is hearing this conversation. Apparently not. Everyone is looking toward the front where the three wise men have just made their entrance to "O, Little Town of Bethlehem." No one seems to have noticed the radiance emanating from the exit sign either. Shit! After all these years of hoping for a religious experience, why does it have to happen in this fundamentalist church? Well, at least it's not Jesus talking to me—not that I have anything against Jesus; I'm just not always wild about the company he keeps.

"I don't get it," I say to my new mother.

"You don't have to get it," the resounding voice answers. "You don't have to have faith, become as a child, or squeeze through the eye of a needle. Here I am. Your true soul mother. That's all."

Then, laughter, starting with a chuckle and ending with something of earthquake proportions. I catch sight of my new mother's face. She has green eyes and full lips, emphasized with bright red lipstick. She is wearing blue eyeshadow. She has the face of a woman who has been around the block *and* over the hill. Her hair looks bleached.

"Are you cheap?" I ask.

"Honey, I'm not cheap. I'm free," she bellows. The image expands. A very big woman, she is reclining against the Stars of the Pleiades, her rich silken garments wafting gently with the breeze. But would there be a breeze so far out there among the Stars of the Pleiades?

"Don't worry about it," the voice says. "Relax."

With that command, I realize how tense my neck and shoulders are. In that moment of realization, my whole body relaxes. A vibrant, pulsing warmth soothes and surrounds me. I see the minister, the choir, the congregation, from a vantage point somewhere near the ceiling in the center of the building. I see the organist's hands move with agility from chord to chord across the keys, his feet unerringly driving the pedals. But the music I'm hearing is beyond the capabilities of even that glorious instrument. The music, the congregation, the choir, everyone—we are all part of a divine oneness.

Poke, poke. Poke, poke. I plunk back down into my body, on the pew next to my carnal mother.

"You'd better take me to the toilet," she says, giving me another poke.

I take her by the arm and guide her as quietly as possible to the door under the radiant exit sign. We take baby steps. Mom stops and turns to say something. She can no longer walk and talk at the same time.

"I'm sorry but I guess when you've got to go, you've got to go." She makes a tight little laughing sound.

"It's just around the corner, Mom," I whisper, guiding her along. I open the door to the restroom and gesture toward one of the stalls. Thank God she can still manage to use the toilet on her own.

"Goddess!" a voice booms in my head.

"Huh?"

"Thank Goddess," is the harmonic response.

"Oh, yeah," I smile.

On the way home, the two women say what they always say. How beautifully Mike sang. How wonderful the sermon. Why, you could hear every word he said. He doesn't mumble like some of those young preachers.

As predictable as that all is, there are equally unpredictable things going on. The warmth of another being fills the spaces of the car and encloses me in an ethereal cocoon—not that I can't see the road, or hear my carnal mother and aunt, but I am cushioned by a cloud of . . . what? Peace? Love? Harmony? No. It's something more than can be described by the lyrics from "Hair." Whatever it is, it is deep within me. It encompasses me. It is better than good.

There's a scent, too. A combination of vanilla, licorice and Cherry-A-Let: a long-forgotten candy bar, the sudden memory of which causes my mouth to water. Lights and colors are brighter but at the same time, less distinct, as if edges and boundaries have softened. All I can relate this to are stories of drug experiences, or my Aunt Ruth's promise to me that if I would only get saved, I would experience the "peace that passeth understanding."

"What's happening?" my inner voice asks.

"Plenty," comes the answer.

"Am I going crazy?"

"Stop with the worrying," bubbles the harmonic laughter.

I take Aunt Hazel home first, then take Mom back to Scripps Home and walk her to her room.

"What will I do now?" she asks, wringing her hands,

"Go to bed, probably. It's a little past ten."

"So late?" she whines, then begins her ritual of worries. "I don't know where my nightgown is. Where will I put my teeth? How will I know when to get up in the morning?"

"It's okay, Mom," I say, showing her the nightgown that is draped across the bed. "I'll get a nurse to come help you get ready for bed."

"But what about in the morning? Can't you stay with me?"

"No, I told Mike I'd meet him at the Ritz-Carlton. I'll phone in the morning."

"But what if the phone isn't working?"

"Then I'll stop by." One of the aides comes to help my mother get ready for bed and I make my break.

I find Mike near the cocktail lounge. He's sitting on a plush couch in front of a fireplace, sipping wine and eating macadamia nuts. I feel a rush of love as he stands to greet me, kissing me with salty lips.

"How was the music?"

"Wonderful," I say, thinking of the thousand-octaved major chords which emanated from beyond the Grand Pleiades.

"How was my solo?"

There was so much going on that I hadn't even noticed Mike's solo, but I'd rather not say so. I'm spared that confession by the waiter's timely appearance.

"Would you care for something to drink? Or something from our bar menu?"

The word Chardonnay is nearly out of my mouth when a harmonic voice suggests a martini.

"I'll have a martini," I say. " Dry. Up with an olive."

"A martini?" Mike says, laughing. "Your mother must have pushed you right over the edge tonight."

"Close," I say. I consider telling him of my Goddess experience, but maybe I should get to know her better before I introduce Mike to his new mother-in-law. I caress the smooth roundness of the glass, the delicate rim, then lift it to my lips. What is more refined than a martini glass? I breathe the medicinal scent of gin, which mellows to the Goddess aroma on the next intake. I catch a subtle, reflective glow of purple and red radiating from the translucent glass. We, the three of us, sit in companionable silence while I absorb the beauty and goodness of life into my being.

Monday morning I awaken early. I lie quietly, sensing the warm, soft, big bosomed presence of the Grand Goddess of the Harmonic Universe. Mike stirs.

"Um, you're so warm," he says, snuggling. I wonder if the warmth of the goddess is expanding?

When I stop to see my mother on my way home from school on Tuesday, worn from working to impart wisdom to the resistant, I sit in the parking lot for a few minutes, gathering strength. Not that it's an awful place—it's bright and airy, always clean and fresh smelling. There's plenty of activity, and laughter. Still . . . I often have to stare at the trees before I can get out of my car and walk up the steps.

"Let's go," the melodic voice of the universe says.

I get out of the car. "Do you have a name? Like, are you maybe the Christina Child?"

"No way. My mother wasn't a virgin. I'm not a virgin. And I'm not a martyr."

Do the nurses and attendants hear euphonic laughter bouncing from the walls, echoing down the halls? They seem not to.

"Mimi Avocada's my full name, but you can just call me Mimi."

"Who named you?"

"I just came with it. It fits. Sometimes I spell it backwards. You know, the great I M, I M?"

I no longer listen to talk radio when driving. Instead I engage in lengthy conversations with my real mother. Stopped for a red light on my way to school one morning I ask, "What did you think of me as a child?"

"I loved you from the moment of your conception."

"Why didn't you introduce yourself earlier?'

"I was always around, you just didn't recognize me. Sometimes you thought I was someone else."

"Like when? Who did I think you were?"

"What's your earliest dream?"

"I don't know."

"Think about it." A whirl of purples and reds, scent of vanilla/licorice/Cherry-a-Let, major chords from below sea level to Himalayan peaks mutate to the sound of a loudly blasting horn and I drive on.

That evening, after dinner with Mike, and phone calls to parents of wayward students, and dozing off during the ten o'clock news, I drag myself to bed and think back to Mimi's question about my earliest dream. In that nearly-asleep-but-not-quite space, it comes to me: the dream of Jesus pushing me in a swing—that wonderful, gentle push. I hurl a question out toward the Pleiades.

"What does that dream have to do with you?"

"I told you," come the booming harmonies. "I was always around, you just didn't recognize me.

"Are you saying you were Jesus?"

"Never! Get it straight. I don't do the martyr thing."

"Well?"

"Well, I'd been watching you. Esther took good care of your bodily needs. That's natural for a carnal mother. But your spirit . . . Remember what she always told you whenever you asked questions about God?"

"Stop bothering me with such silly questions," I say, surprising myself that I still remember feeling hurt over such a long ago slight.

"I thought you needed a lift," Mimi says.

"So why didn't *you* give me one?"

"It wouldn't have meant much right then. I have an in with many symbolic figures. Jesus seemed like a good choice for the time. I knew you'd recognize him."

"You mean you *sent* Jesus?"

"Let's just say we've got sort of a reciprocal agreement going—Jesus, Isis, Buddha, Santa

Claus, Mary the Virgin, Kali, Muhammed, the Tooth Fairy."

As I pull into the school parking lot I tell Mimi that I could use some help during first period.

"Javier's going to be absent today. First period will be smooth as silk," she says, swirling her garments. "I'm going to hang with the sisters for a while, but remember 'Lo, I am with you always, even unto the end.'"

"Plagiarizing Jesus?" I ask.

"Nope, just another reciprocal agreement," she laughs. Pure tones and full harmonies ease me into the classroom.

~

Now, decades after the first Mimi appearance, she still sometimes glides down from her perch in the Pleiades, bringing peace, and humor and comfort, reminding me that the universe is harmonic.

So . . . what does all this mean? Is Mimi simply a figment of my imagination? If so, what purpose does she fulfill? But those are questions that exist in a concrete, literal world. Not that there's anything wrong with that world, but there are other worlds, and Mimi offers a means of access to other worlds. Jesus, Allah, Krishna, Mimi, all of the holy metaphors offer access to other worlds. I'm sticking with Mimi.

Firsts & Lasts

After nearly a year of stay-at-home restrictions, things have piled up. Three bags of plastics to go to the recycle bin outside Save-Mart. Several bags of clothing to be donated to a thrift store. A stack of clothing that needs to be dry cleaned, though since I've mainly lived in top to bottom sweats, the dry cleaning items are fewer than they would have been for a comparable period in "normal life."

Between home deliveries and curb pick-up, I've been inside the grocery store only three times in the past eleven months, and then just to race in and out for some crucial necessity—wine, say, or heavy cream, no leisurely browsing, no squeezing avocados until the just-right one is found. Zip in, zip out, holding my breath as long as possible.

Ah, but today, now that I have received both shots of the Pfizer vaccine and waited the appropriate time for my immunity to kick in, I load the car with the year's collections, pack my tote with hand sanitizer and wipes, drape a mask around my neck, and set out. Such errands that have, for a lifetime of adulthood, been experienced as drudgery, a have-to list to drag through before getting to the real business of life—these same errands are now welcome adventures!

Even though her habitually bright smile is hidden beneath a mask, it's good to see the friendly cashier at Save-On Cleaners; good to watch the careful counting as she pulls each item (blouses, pants, bedspread) one at a time from the dusty trash bag. I witness anew the wonder of the clothing-crowded motorized track delivering up another customer's order from somewhere in the mysterious back of the building.

Next is the drop-off of clothing at St. Vincent De Paul. I'm not Catholic and I hope my contribution will go toward helping the poor and not get siphoned into some wacko anti-abortion fund. If I were more dedicated to living my values, I'd drive across town to the Women's Alliance donation center, but convenience wins out. I also use too much plastic and am a sloppy recycler. Other than that, though, I'm a good person.

The most exciting part of today's outing is a trip to the Lazy Boy furniture store. I've long wanted a comfortable reading chair to go in front of my living room window where the light is good throughout the day. Plus if I want to remain a member in good standing of the old-old club, it's time to get myself a recliner. From reading chair, to napping chair, to bed when the traditional bed becomes too hard to get in and out of, recliners are as necessary to my age group today as hoop skirts were to us in the '50s.

At Lazy Boy a heavy tasseled rope is strung across the entrance. A masked salesman, James, unhooks the rope to invite me in, then reattaches it as I enter. Together we amble toward the middle of the showroom, where there are hundreds and hundreds of chairs in all variety of sizes, shapes and colors—so many choices. But wait! Whatever happened to wrought iron? The first chair I ever bought with my first husband back in 1956 had a wrought iron back and legs and even with a cushion it was uncomfortable, but we liked the style. The chair lasted longer than the husband . . .

"Give this one a try," James says, gesturing toward a comfortable looking but massive chair. I tell him my living room is small. I don't want any thing bulky and I have budget restrictions. He points toward a fairly narrow chair with curved wooden arms. No, I don't want bulky, but I do want padded arms. I also want it to swivel so I can face the TV or a visitor on the couch across the room.

As James leads me toward a chair he thinks I'll like, we walk past displays of room groupings, each with matching couch and chair, or paired chairs, brightened by colorful pillows. There's always a lamp, coffee table, decorative pieces artfully displayed. A strong desire to totally redecorate my living room lodges somewhere between heart and head until reality quickly overcomes desire.

The sad last five years of my dementia-stricken husband's life totally emptied our retirement savings. My teacher's retirement covers the basics, but no room do-overs are in my future. I remind myself that, even though it's large for the room, I love the long leather couch my husband and I bought together back when he was fully himself, back when we had the illusion of financial security. I love the darkened patina at the top of the corner cushion, where he rested his head while watching TV.

"You may like this one," James says, gesturing toward a non-bulky recliner that is on sale. "Try it."

I take a seat. James shows me how to automatically change the angle of the back rest and the position of the footrest. I discover on my own that the seat of the chair can quickly go up and down, expanding and contracting when I press two buttons at the same time. I'd like a little excitement in my life and think it might be worth it to pay the extra fee for the automatic controls. James leads me toward the back where several large round tables are set up. I sit across from him as he starts to write up an order—"just to see where we stand on this."

If I order the chair with the ugly scratchy fabric as shown I can get it for the sale price of $649. Custom fabric will be $300 to $900 more. I don't want ugly-scratchy. I choose better fabric for a $349 add-on price. Even though I won't be getting the sale price for the chair, it turns out that everything in the store is 10% off. For a limited time only, of course.

The mechanical controls are an added $500. I guess I'll give up the cheap thrills. I remind him that I want a swivel, which is another $100, plus installation. He doesn't know how much the installation will be. That's a different department.

With add-ons, plus tax, it comes to $1,200 and some change. It's a stretch but I will, after all, have it for the rest of my life. I sign the order form. James checks the factory schedule. The chair will be delivered within six months he tells me.

Six months?? I'm old!

"I don't think so," I tell James, and I draw a line through my signature.

Across the showroom I spot a chair in the same style as the one I've just declined, but with a leather fabric. A floor model, it's significantly less than the total on the unsigned order.

"Let's look at that one," I say to James, motioning in the direction of the chair I've just spotted. On sale for $799. The one I'm *not* going to buy is my preferred color, which, according to the tag, is called "buff" (or to those of us who still think of colors in less high-sounding terms, light beige). The color of the $799 chair is "gravity," translated to light gray for the over-eighty crowd. For my room I prefer beige to gray, but for a $300 difference and immediate possession? Grey starts looking better and better. There's a tiny ballpoint pen mark on the left arm.

"Can this be cleaned off?" I ask James.

"Let's see," he says, walking toward the back of the store.

He returns with a soft cloth and a bottle of Lazy Boy brand leather cleaner. He squeezes a dollop of cleaner on the cloth, rubs lightly on the spot, then freezes.

"Oh, no!" he says. "It's degrading the leather!"

I take a close look. The spot is gone. I don't see a difference in the leather. Maybe it's slightly duller? I can't tell.

"This is awful!" James says, examining the bottle more carefully and turning the cloth from one side to the other. "It shouldn't do that! Our cleaning brand, our fabric, it should be totally safe!" He shakes his head. "I couldn't possibly sell this chair to you now."

I look again.

"It's not really noticeable," I say to him.

"To me it is. I feel awful about this. I need to get this chair off the floor."

I rub my thumb across the spot. I'm not great at estimating measurements but my guess is that it's half an inch in diameter. Plus it's nearly invisible.

"I still like the chair," I tell him, sitting back down in it.

He shakes his head, defeated. I feel sorry for him. We sit in silence, James staring off at the ceiling.

"Maybe with an added 15% discount?" he says.

"That works for me."

"I just have to check with my manager but the flaw is obviously my fault."

Another trip to the back of the store while I sit rocking, perusing the throw pillows decorating every couch and side chair in the show room. Maybe a pair of bright new pillows plus the recliner is enough of a do-over.

James returns with a thumbs up.

"Don't forget the swivel," I say, as I watch him enter details on a new order form.

When he reaches the line for "delivery charges," he asks, "Will it fit in your car? No need to pay for delivery if you don't have to."

"The back seats will lay flat," I tell him. He draws a line through "delivery charge."

When the paperwork is finished and signed, the credit card run and approved, James wraps the chair in plastic. I prepare the trunk and drive the car back to receiving. In moments the big steel door creaks open. James and another man wheel my new, now-$679, chair out on a dolly and carefully wedge it into the trunk.

"Do you have someone to help you get the chair out?" he asks.

"I'll find someone," I assure him.

~

Later in the day, after I've rearranged the other furniture, a friend brings the chair in for me. I sit half-reclined, half-dozing, and wonder at the process of buying a chair, wonder how many chairs have I bought in my lifetime? How many tables? Lamps? Rugs? My first husband and I bought our first chair the week before we married. We split the costs. It fit in the trunk of First's 1955 Customline Ford: two-tone with a black body and white top. It was a short drive to Temple City, then down a private drive to the one-bedroom apartment we would live in after the wedding, an apartment conveniently located just behind Mr. Burger's.

I walked ahead and unlocked the door while my new husband carried the chair up the stairs and into the small living room. It went well with our already installed couch. We were pleased with our first chair purchase.

Unlike that time of firsts (first chair, first apartment, first wedding, first house, first baby), this is a time of lasts. This is the last chair I will ever buy. The last car I will ever buy is parked in my driveway. My last trip to Europe was in 2008. Other lasts have occurred, unremarked upon at the time: last time to catch a wave in the cold Pacific at a beach in Southern California, last time to do a set of jumping jacks, last time to speak on the phone with my Canadian friend, last time to have sex with my now dead husband, and so many other lasts to come before I breathe my last breath.

I lean the chair back to full recline, ready for the first nap I will ever take in this last chair. It's good to notice the rare firsts when they come my way.

Healthy Aging in Action

Yesterday, zipping west along J street toward the H Street Bridge--or wait, is it the J Street Bridge? Since I have driven this same route nearly every day for the past six years, it seems like something I should know. But I don't. Anyway, zipping west along J Street toward the bridge, I see an ancient couple trudging along the grassy edge of the roadway to my right. He is walking on the street side, carrying a nearly full Safeway bag in his left arm, and holding his companion's hand with his right hand.

It looks like it's not an easy walk for this pair of ancients (probably only ten or so years younger than I), and I think maybe I should loop around and offer them a ride. I think about it for so long I miss the last possible turn off. I could make a U-turn at Sac State, after the bridge, drive back to Howe, make another U-turn, pull over beside them and offer them a ride.

They're probably walking back to Campus Commons, that retirement community on Cadillac Drive. But doesn't Campus Commons offer van service to grocery stores? And don't they provide meals? What did these old farts need at Safeway, anyway? Campus Commons is directly across the street from Raley's, so is it worth heat stroke and exhaustion just to save a few pennies at Safeway?

Maybe they're not Campus Commons people. Maybe they live in that apartment complex just down the street from Campus Commons, the one I moved into after Mike went to memory care. The one I moved into after being between places, from one hard place to another, furniture stored, necessities in my car, nomad-ing from relative to friend to relative, not exactly homeless but perhaps fitting the "unhomed" euphemism. Maybe that's where they're headed, to the Cadillac Drive apartment complex.

Maybe they *want* to be walking, it's part of their effort to meet the requirement for one of the Four Pillars of Healthy Aging—Exercise. And maybe what's in the cumbersome bag will take care of another of the Four Pillars—good Nutrition. And they're holding hands. Pillar number three—Connection. And number four: Purpose? Well, they've obviously got a destination.

I forgo the left lane and take the right turn into my neighborhood. I've got things to do. They're fine. If I see them again, some other time, I'll pull over and offer them a ride.

Years ago, when Mike was still Mike and I was still pre-archaic, whenever he saw an old couple crossing the street together, he would say, "That will be us someday." Sometimes his remark seemed sad, other times funny. Whatever the mood conveyed, I never questioned the truth of it. Such expectations.

Because I was five years older than Mike, it seemed likely that we'd take our leave near the same time—that his prediction when sighting old couples walking together would come true. But likely is not reality and expectations often turn out to be fantasies. And though I rarely revisit those old expectations of mine, seeing the walkers on this day leaves my left hand feeling cold and empty, the hand that would have been held, had we been the walkers, had I not been driving home to an unexpected solo, yet not unhappy, life.

From Then to Now

Early on it was who liked whom and who didn't, and how to talk to boys ("always ask them about their interests—football, baseball, cars.") Then it was who was going steady and soon it was who got engaged, and weddings, and quick and easy casseroles. Who was pregnant, whose kid was smart, or had asthma, or was still running around in diapers at the age of two. Then it was the PTA, and maybe part time jobs while the kids were in school, or in pursuit of a long delayed career. At parties—the men in the living room or den, we women in the kitchen—in both rooms, the talk often started with "When the kids are grown . . ."

There was the Civil Rights movement, and Vietnam, and an awareness that our nation was not as heroic and pure in spirit as it had seemed to be when we were growing up during The War. There was *The Feminine Mystique* and *Our Bodies, Ourselves*. Consciousness raising groups and assertiveness training brought different insights, maybe resentments, to the conversation. Somewhere along the way talk turned to who got divorced and why, and then the married kids, gay kids, grandkids lost to electronic devices, retirement, our own parents needing help.

Now it's who has moved to assisted living, or has been diagnosed with a serious illness, or can no longer carry on a conversation, or who has died. And being old. We talk a lot about the surprising condition of oldness. In addition to the inevitable decay of body and mind there is, for many of us, invisibility, loneliness, isolation.

But as frustrating as invisibility can be when waiting to be noticed or served in a restaurant, it has its advantages. A group of old women drinking wine or beer at a picnic table in a public park goes unnoticed. It's easy to eavesdrop at the local Starbuck's. The invisibility of the old could be a plus if we wanted to pursue criminal activities.

Appalled by the inhumane treatment of immigrants at our southern borders, six of us elders in a spiritual growth group figured we would never come under suspicion were #45 to be assassinated. Even if we were caught, how long could a life sentence be for us? Since none of us knew how to handle a weapon, maybe poison in his Big Mac would be the way to go? Rather than reading and discussing the scheduled spiritual growth materials, we spent a few meetings working on the details: where and how to switch out the Big Mac, what poison would be best, where to stay in D.C., etc. Ultimately though, we decided to put our plan on hold until after the election, and turned our attention back to growing spiritually.

~

I'm not often afflicted with a sense of loneliness and isolation. I do have, though, a particular loneliness that comes with the loss of a partner. I am no longer the most important person in the world to anyone. I miss the warmth of a sleeping body next to mine, and that early morning, half-awake, expression of love that starts the day. That said, for more than seven years, when Mike was caught in the throes of dementia, I longed for the partner-less aloneness I now have.

Like many women of my generation, I went from my parents' home to the home I shared with my first husband, to the rental I shared as a single mom with my two young daughters, to homes with my second husband and kids, then just with him, minus any kids at home. It was not until 2011, at the age of seventy-six, that I moved into a small apartment and began a solo life.

Barring the occasional longing for a man in my bed and the inconvenience of not having someone to stick their finger on the knot of a package I'm trying to tie, I'm pretty well suited to living alone. I can read in bed with the light on, and write without interruption, and eat whatever I want, whenever I want, with my fingers. For me, alone more often means convenience than it means loneliness or invisibility.

My So-Called Spiritual Journey—Part 2

New York Times columnist John Leland, who has chronicled six old-old New Yorkers over the past seven years, writes: "For those who make it to old-old age, there remains the challenge: How do you make a full and meaningful life when you can't do so many of the things you once did? At the end of life, what turns out to really matter, and what is just noise?"

At this stage of life, a search for meaning is not new to me. Throughout my adulthood I've experienced a "full and meaningful life" loving, caring for, and engaging with family, spouse and friends. There was purpose and meaning throughout my professional teaching career, and then with ongoing volunteer teaching. I knew I was making a small difference in the lives of at least some of the people in my realm and that was fulfilling. In later adulthood, I also found meaning and purpose in writing for teens and adults. Working with organizations that were doing good work in the broader world also added to my sense of purpose. Now, as both bodily and mental competence is gradually, or maybe suddenly, diminishing, what will bring meaning and purpose to my life?

~

In 2012, shortly after *Over 70 and I Don't Mean MPH* was released, I gave a reading at the Odd Fellows retirement community in Walla Walla, Washington. One of the segments I chose to read described my spiritual journey (as you can read in Part One of this essay).

The youngest two people in the room the day of that reading were a couple from Indiana, probably in their early fifties, in town visiting the husband's mother, a resident at the Odd Fellows Home. Afterward, they came over to chat with me.

"We kept expecting you to say you were a Unitarian Universalist when you were reading about your spiritual journey," the man said. "You are, aren't you?"

I shook my head.

"You sound like a UU. You should check it out," he advised.

They bought two books and introduced me to his mother. They were soon on their way, but their question lingered. What probably led them to suspect me of Unitarian Universalist leanings was the part about the connections of all living creatures, and our interdependence. That, and an acceptance that there are no concrete answers to what comes next. Because there wasn't time for a leisurely conversation, I didn't tell the couple how on the nose was their perception of my compatibility with UU principles.

I'd had a long, but sporadic, history with Unitarian Universalism. My upbringing had been mostly mainstream Protestantism with a bit of fire and brimstone fundamentalism tossed in. Although as a youngster I tried (who doesn't want to go to heaven?), I could never quite suspend enough disbelief to be a good Christian.

As an adult, I'd wanted my young daughters to gain a foundation of the moral and ethical teachings and sense of community that comes with church involvement, and I could appreciate being part of a church community, but as a non-believer I could never fully belong. I continued to ponder matters of the spirit, though without the help—or restrictions—of organized religion.

Sometime in the early 80s, I attended a talk given by Norman Cousins on his then-recent book, *Anatomy of an Illness as Perceived by the Patient: Reflections on Healing and Regeneration* and on the healing power of laughter. The site of his talk was the Throop Memorial Unitarian Universalist Church in Pasadena, a large, imposing structure with stained glass windows, burnished wooden pews, and a general sense of formality.

While waiting for Cousins to appear I took a hymnal from the back of the pew in front of me and began thumbing through. The hymns held no mention of Jesus. There was a smattering of "God"s here and there but no "God the Father." In the front of the book was a list of Unitarian Universalist Principles, among them affirmations of the inherent worth and dignity of every person, respect for the interdependent web of all existence, the goal of world community with peace, liberty, and justice for all. Here was a church I could fully embrace! I didn't though, since I was then attending a local Episcopal church where Mike was on the staff as tenor soloist. But the feeling of inclusiveness that came with that brief exposure to UU principles stayed with me.

When Mike left his soloist job at the Episcopal church, I suggested we visit Neighborhood Church, another UU church in Pasadena. Again, I resonated with the UU principles and practices. Mike also liked Neighborhood Church and we attended as a family for a year or so. As teenagers, the girls' attendance was sporadic, but Mike, five-year-old Matt, and I were regulars. Mike sang in the choir. I, along with others, taught the high school group. But when Mike took a job as tenor soloist at a large Presbyterian church in Hollywood, I shifted from Sundays at Neighborhood Church to leisurely Sunday mornings at home with the *Los Angeles Times.*

In 1998 after we moved from the L.A. area to Sacramento, we went church shopping. Mike was wanting a church with a strong music program, preferably with a children's choir that could include the grandkids. I was more concerned with the theology. After a year or so of dipping into various Sacramento churches, we became regular attendees, then members, of the Unitarian

Universalist Society of Sacramento. When we joined UUSS there was not a strong music program. After our first year there, Mike became the music director, and set about building the program he'd hoped to find when we were on the church search.

Again, I resonated with UU theology and soon felt at home at UUSS. I was involved with a writing group, a book group, and one of a series of small group programs designed to strengthen community. That lasted for five or so years until Mike, tired of the demands of the job, resigned. As is generally the case with most churches, when a paid leader leaves—a minister, music director, religious education director, etc.—policy requires that they not attend services for some period of time so that their replacement will not have to compete with the previous leader and his/her followers.

When the Odd Fellows couple called attention to my UU leanings it had been seven years since I'd attended a UU service, or any other service for that matter. But the seed was planted. I fully subscribed to the principles of Universal Unitarianism so why wasn't I connecting with a congregation? Supporting an institution for which I held great respect?

In July of 2014, two years after the Odd Fellows *Over 70 . . .* reading, I again visited a Unitarian Universalist Society of Sacramento service. I was cordially welcomed by those I'd known in the past, by those who had sung with Mike, and also by others not known to me. I don't remember the topic of the sermon that day, or what music was sung. What I do remember is that the experience was both comforting and thought-provoking, that it gave me a broader lens through which to view the world and all its troubles, and that I was among warmhearted people doing good work in the world.

I soon became a regular attendee, re-upped my membership, and have since served on several committees, led small, spiritual-deepening groups, and generally participated in the life of the congregation. My understanding of the mysteries of the universe and eternity has not changed much since my reconnection to UUSS. What has changed is that I'm giving more thought to matters of the spirit than I had in previous decades. And giving voice on Sundays to the UUSS mission, "We come together to deepen our lives and be a force for healing in the world," reminds me that I have a broader purpose than simply doing the laundry, buying groceries, paying bills, and watering the plants on my patio.

In this time of great political divisions, a time when it seems ignorant, angry liars are determined to turn our democracy upside down, I am particularly challenged by the first UU Principle which affirms "the inherent worth and dignity of every person." It's difficult to assign worth and dignity to the anti-vaxxers, the Biden-win deniers—a task I wouldn't even attempt were it not for being part of the UUSS community—but I find it's a worthy, if not always successful, effort.

John Leland asks, "How do you make a meaningful life when you can't do so many things that you once did? And what turns out to really matter?" For me, connections with family and friends matter. I find meaning through writing, and through occasionally leading writing workshops. Communications with readers, knowing that one of my books has made a difference to them, reminds me that my work matters.

Beyond the everyday stuff of life, there are the universal mysteries. As my individual end of life approaches, I find that UU principles, along with the UUSS community, offer a foundation for the consideration of the big picture. Many thanks to the anonymous couple at that 2012 Odd Fellows reading who reminded me of my Unitarian Universalist leanings.

Ashes to Ashes

These days, many of us widows and widowers—mostly widows—have a box of cremains stashed on a high shelf in a seldom used closet, or in a decorative urn on the mantle. One friend has an expensive necklace with a jewel made from her husband's pressed cremains. Says she never takes it off. Sometimes I think that she loves that necklace more than she loved the living breathing husband.

Mike's ashes are in a plastic box labeled Human Cremains. It sits on a high shelf in the garage, next to back-up supplies of paper towels, laundry soap, toilet paper, and wine. I'm not one of those women who thinks their dead husband is watching from above and judging their behavior, but I know Mike would not want his final destination to be on a shelf in the garage. So I've arranged to give him a more fitting resting place or, more accurately, resting places.

This morning my task is to scrub the labels off the tea containers destined to contain portions of Mike's ashes. Four cylindrical tins of Ambessa African Tea Blend at $4.99 apiece; four more square tins of Zhena's Gypsy Tea Coconut Chai at $5.99 each. About $44 in total for the cremains' penultimate resting places. A much better deal than the

$199 silver urn recommended by the cremation service.

I doubt that either Gypsy Coconut Chai or Ambessa African Tea will ever take precedence over the bags of black tea in the classic Lipton's yellow box that can always be found in my cupboard. I'll admit, though, that both types of these more elevated tea bags have nice aromas. Now safely stored in zip-locked baggies, they wait for a time when some visitor with more discerning taste wants a cup of something not Lipton's.

I fill the dishpan with scalding water and immerse the tea tins into a label-soaking bath. Later in the evening, after the tins are cleaned and label free, I spread the now rarely-used lace tablecloth onto my dining room table. I take one of Mike's favorite Waterford wine glasses from the top shelf. How unlike the cheap K-Mart glass which I often fill to the brim with cheap wine. I pour an appropriate measure of a better Chardonnay into the glass and take a sip.

I start the Arthur Rubinstein CD of Chopin waltzes—our favorite of all the CDs we played over and over when I was pregnant with my youngest, the son who was ours together. According to the wisdom of the time, the fetus was influenced by the sounds he/she heard in utero, so every day from the second trimester on, he was exposed to Chopin, Mozart, Bach. The process expanded *my* appreciation of the greats; however, by the time that child was fourteen, he was deep into heavy metal and punk.

The crystal, the tablecloth, the music—the entire setting is so appropriately Mike. I get the box of cremains, a small scoop, a clean jar that once held pink grapefruit slices (light sugar), and arrange them on the table with the tea tins.

Another sip of wine. From the outer box I remove and open the sealed plastic bag of ashes. As described in the cremation service brochure, the contents are grayish in color, with a coarse sandy texture. Also as described, there are small bone fragments. I hold the beveled stem of the leaded crystal wine glass, lift it to the light, catch a pastel prism, remembering Mike's care of these glasses. How after all of the dinner guests were gone and I was in bed, he would gently wash the crystal in warm sudsy water, carefully dry each glass with a linen dishcloth, then place them back on their designated shelf in the china cabinet.

Left to my own devices, I would never have spent that much money on crystal glasses. Unlike now, though, I wasn't often left to my own devices. Another swallow of wine. Two. From the plastic bag I scoop ashes into the grapefruit jar. One scoop for Matt, the heavy metal/punk rock lover, to take with him to Vienna, one of Mike's favorite places. One to go to Mike's brother, Jerry, in Florida, to be scattered at the family plot, around their grandmother, mother, father, a baby sister, a beloved cousin. Jerry will also set a plaque among them with Mike's name and dates. Another scoop for me to later toss into the waters of Shaw's Cove in Laguna Beach. I put the jar in the Human Cremains box, the box back in its place in the garage where those ashes can safely rest until they reach their final Vienna, Florida, Shaw's Cove destinations.

I divide the remaining cremains evenly into the tea tins, make sure the lids are secure, and place them in a canvas tote bag, ready for tomorrow's trip to San Francisco. I double-check the list to be sure I have enough for everyone: Dale, Marg, Corry, Sharon, Doug, Subei, Lena, me. Eight.

~

By 3:00 we're all settled into our rooms at San Francisco's Inn at the Opera near Davies Hall. Mike and I often stayed here when we came to the city for a San Francisco Symphony event. We have dinner at another of Mike's favorite places, Jardiniere, just blocks away from the hotel. After dinner, we play charades, in honor of Mike. If there had been an Olympics charades event, Mike would have been a gold medal winner. Charades is always fun with our group, but tonight's game is diminished by Mike's absence, by his missing antics.

In bed by 10:30, I open *Americanah* to my marked page. I'm determined to broaden my usual reading scope beyond American and British writers. In the past year I've read books by Indian, Vietnamese, and Swedish writers. *Americanah* will be the first I've read by a Nigerian writer, Chimamanda Ngozi Adichie. It's an embarrassment to me that I'm halfway through the book and I still can't remember her name. I say it three times, hoping this time it sticks.

After a few minutes of trying and failing to pay attention to what I'm reading, I close the book and gaze about the room. A queen-size bed with a gold brocade spread, fresh white sheets and pillowcases, wall-mounted reading lamps above each side of the bed. Against the wall facing the bed is a bench upholstered in blue velvet. A window looks out onto Fulton St. The hotel has been refurbished since Mike and I were here . . . when? I count back. Mike was diagnosed with Fronto-temporal Dementia in 2009, but much was going wrong before that. Was it 2007 when we last came to the symphony? 2006? Probably 2006. At least ten years ago. Michael Tilson Thomas was conducting that day but I don't remember who the featured musicians were. A very young pianist, I think.

Mike had already begun being overly anxious about getting places on time and we took our seats in Davies Hall much earlier than needed. Shortly after we sat down, he became impatient for the music to start. Squirmy, bordering on angry. Luckily, it was not long before a woman squeezed past us and took the seat on his other side. She was chatty and his long practiced social skills kicked in. Once the music started, he was his old attentive self.

I doubt that I thought then, "This is the last time I will ever come to such a performance with Mike." When we crawled into bed that night in this hotel, I doubt I thought, "This is the last time I will ever spend the night here with Mike." I was well into the time of lasts. I just hadn't realized it yet. Now, though, I know this is the last time I will ever stay in this hotel; tonight's dinner was the last I'll ever eat at Jardiniere. At eighty-one, I can't help recognizing the lasts.

Our plan is to scatter Mike's ashes around several of his beloved San Francisco sites—Grace Cathedral, the Legion of Honor, and Golden Gate Park. Grace Cathedral is closest to the hotel so we start there. It is a cold and drizzly morning as we stand huddled together on the lower steps of the iconic Gothic church. I hand the tea tins around. We talk about the rest of the day, the rain, driving the wet streets to our next destinations, more parking searches, and decide to limit today's scattering to the cathedral grounds. We agree to gather at a bench near the labyrinth, then walk off in separate directions, our tins in hand.

Mike loved Grace Cathedral, the beauty of the building, the stained glass windows, the acoustics, the organization's ongoing work for social justice. It's an appropriate setting for today's dispersal. I make my way to the garden and follow a path that curves through lush greenery to the other side of the property. I'm no gardener. The only person who brought plants into our yards or patios was Mike and out of the hundreds of plants he provided over the years I can name just a few. Azaleas. Impatiens. Roses. I wander through the rose garden, wondering which of the roses might be one of his favorites. We both liked Mr. Lincoln, a deep red that actually smells like a rose. I remember when he planted a Mr. Lincoln in the border between our fence and driveway.

The bushes aren't labeled and the roses won't be blooming for another few months so there's no way to tell a Mr. Lincoln from a John Wilkes Booth, or a Mary Todd, or whatever else is in this garden of roses. I walk the rows, looking for a healthy specimen. They all look healthy. Bare branches, but healthy. I pause near the middle of the rose garden. Mike always liked to be in the middle of things. I shake a few ashes onto the ground, take a few deep breaths, and wander off.

Up a slight incline is a row of azaleas. That's one of the few plants I can recognize even when they're not flowering. I sprinkle a few more ashes at the base of an azalea. Another sprinkle at the base of a shade tree, another near a statue of St. Francis of Assisi, and my tin is empty. I grab a handful of leaves from a nearby fern, wipe the tin free of any ash residue, pull my scarf closer around my neck, and return to the labyrinth.

I leave my empty tin beside the bench, bury my hands deeper in the side pockets of my jacket, and take the first step into the labyrinth. The smooth surface is still shiny from the earlier drizzle, but the clouds have lifted. I take one slow step after another, deliberately. One change of direction after another. I read somewhere that the way to the center is a time of letting go, releasing, a time to open the heart and quiet the mind. Step. What am I releasing? Step. Well . . . a handful of ashes from the body I loved and lived with for nearly forty years. Step. I don't count those last years when we didn't live together. Step. In truth, I didn't love that body then. Step. He was so goddamned unlovable those last years. Step. Hmmm. I'm probably not achieving an open heart, a quiet mind. Step. But all of those years before FTD. Step. We laughed. Step. We loved. Step. We raised a family. Step. Plenty of ups and downs. Change direction. Step. More ups than downs. Step.

Would it have been more respectful to bury Mike in the ground? Step. Stop it! Step. Stop the second guessing. Step. All along you did the best you could. Step. You're still doing the best you can. Step. It's good enough! Change direction. Step. Stop with the words. Step. Focus on your breath. Step. Feel cool air. Step. Hear the shuffle of feet. Distant traffic sounds. Step. A slow shuffle. Change direction. Step. Step. Change direction. Step. Step . . . It feels natural, these short steps and abrupt changes of direction. It's my life. I suppose that's true for most of us. I suppose that's why labyrinth practices have lasted through centuries.

I pause in the center. Breathe deeply. Feel at peace. Some say this is a time to accept and receive guidance. I don't receive guidance, or if I do, it's too subtle for me to recognize. I do, though, have a renewed awareness of my connection to all that is—well worth the walk.

~

We lunch at the Absinthe Brasserie & Bar, another of Mike's San Francisco favorites. Five of the six adults order vodka martinis, Corry has a Cosmopolitan. Someone in the group ought to have ordered Mike's Ginger Rogers cocktail, but none of us wanted to trade a straight up vodka martini for his favorite sweet gin and lime juice concoction. No one in this group has a daytime drinking habit, but today is worthy of exception. We talk about where each of us left Mike's ashes. Ignoring the hard FTD years, we talk of the Mike we loved—his humor, his life as a singer, his love of silver and china and crystal. Subei remembers playing the piano with him. She remembers that he never missed any of her recitals, or grandparents' days at her school. Corry remembers playing Mad Libs with him when she was maybe six or seven, and how they laughed hysterically over "green fart juice."

A memory comes to me from a time when the kids were still young. Mike and I were out in the backyard, lying naked on the hammock, watching a meteor shower. It was a beautiful night, but when it came time to go in, we found that the door had locked shut behind us. No pockets, no keys. No way were we going to rouse a sleeping kid to come open the door for us. After checking several windows, we found a window into the dining room that was not shut securely. Together we were able to shift and shove the window halfway open and, with a lot of squirming around, Mike managed to squeeze through the narrow opening. He later complained he had endangered his manhood. It would take more than one martini for me to reveal this memory to today's assembled group, but I welcome its secret presence.

~

Within the next few months, Jerry was able to place a portion of Mike's ashes in the family section of a cemetery in Tampa. Matt, in Vienna for a conference, scattered ashes in the Danube. It was a windy day and some of the ashes blew back onto his shoes. It was okay, Matt said, he liked the idea of walking around Vienna with his dad again.

~

In early September, I extend my author's visit to Southern California to include time with long-time friends. The day before I'm to return home, I drive to Laguna Beach and park on Cliff Drive above Shaw's Cove. With beach towel, wallet, iPhone, two 6-oz. bottles of Chardonnay, a long stemmed wineglass, and the last remaining tin of Mike's ashes packed in a tote bag, I start down the stairway between private homes that has long provided public access to the cove. Halfway down I pause to breathe deeply of the cool, salt-tinged air, the lightness of which suddenly conjures the air of other beaches, other times. Back when I was a teething toddler, spirited away by my grandmother from the summer heat of the San Gabriel Valley to a campground at Huntington Beach, to summers at Newport Beach as a child and later as a teen, to so many adult summertime visits to Laguna when my kids were little, and later after they were grown, to times with grandkids, to now, this familiar beach air is a precious gift.

I settle to the left of the stairs near the tide pools. Up closer to the cliffs there are a couple of serious frisbee players. At water's edge opposite the foot of the stairs three kids are building a sandcastle. A few people are splashing around in the water at the other end of the beach. Maybe it's because most schools have started by now. Or maybe it's because it's grey and overcast. Whatever the reason, it's a quiet day at Shaw's Cove.

After spending too long messing around with my iPhone, searching for appropriate music, I decide I don't need background music for this task. I take the tin of ashes, the wineglass, and one of the little Chardonnays from my tote and place them on the beach towel. I pour the wine into the glass and put the empty bottle back in my bag. I know it's illegal to drink wine on the beach; also illegal to toss human cremains into the ocean. If I were younger I'd probably drink my wine from a generic paper cup instead of an easily identifiable wineglass. Maybe I'd take Mike's ashes to a more secluded area at the other end of the tide pools. But the older I get, the less visible I become, so I'm confident my crimes will go unnoticed.

Slowly sipping the wine, my mind wanders from the beach and the history it holds, to Mike and our lives together, to the sometimes still disturbing awareness that he now exists only in memory. I finish my wine, pick up the tea tin, slip off my sandals, and walk to the edge of the shore. The water is shockingly cold as it comes up past my feet to my ankles, then recedes, repeats and recedes, repeats and recedes. In a few steps I'm standing calf deep in the water, watching the pattern of the flow, wanting to be sure the ashes will get carried out to the deep rather than washed back on shore, though does it matter?

With the pull of a receding wave, I cast a wide arc of ashes into the current. Swirling the tin clean in the water at my feet, knowing that all of the ashes have found their destinations, I feel a sudden sense of relief that this job is done, that what's left of Mike is beyond the garage and out in the world where he belongs.

I expect the ashes to sink quickly but instead they gather on the surface, floating in a cluster, gently lifting and falling, all the way out beyond the breakers. I focus on the steadily changing configurations of ashes and the steadily changing configurations of my life, until it is late in the day and I can no longer distinguish ashes from sea.

Grief Stops By

Me: What? Yeah, you can visit for a while. But I can't see you very well. Come in out of the shadows . . . Wait. Who else is with you?

Grief: My family: Father Death. Mother Loss. Sister Disease. Brother Injustice. Cousins Regret, Anger, Disappointment, Resentment . . .

I only invited you.

We stick together—me and my family.

Well . . . come on in. You can come through the living room, but if this is an overnight you'll have to stay in the back room.

The back room? I deserve a better place than your dusty old back room. Why can't I stay in your living room?

I prefer other company.

You can't pretend I don't exist. You can't ignore me. If you ignore me, there will be repercussions, maybe with Sister Disease or Cousin Regret.

Don't threaten me. I'm not ignoring you. I'm simply keeping you where you belong. You don't get to be free-range in my residence. You're only in the living room for a short conversation, because I invited you.

What about your precious goddess? The one you call Mimi? She gets to come and go as she pleases.

I like her better. I prefer Joy to Grief.

You can't truly know joy without knowing grief.

Maybe, but since I know both, I prefer Joy.

I always get a bum rap.

Not really. Plenty of people prefer you to Joy. You make them feel important.

You have to admit that I have influence though. Like the other evening at Kathy's party, and when you wake up in the middle of the night and find me in bed with you . . .

I'll admit there are times when you loom large. Kathy's party, celebrating her seventy years of life, telling stories of our decades of friendship and shared work. Suddenly *you* shoved your way in, forcing me to feel the emptiness that is Mike's absence. The pure tenor voice, absent from the

Happy Birthday song. The silly antics of Mike's famous party Hokey-Pokey, absent. For a moment,
in the midst of warmth and laughter, you and
emptiness were my only reality.

*It's taken a long time for you to recognize me. When
your father died, I couldn't even get through the
door, much less find a place in your living room.*

I was busy with the cousins: Anger, Disappointment, Abandonment . . .

*You had all those armed guards around you with
special instructions to keep me out.*

Yes. Well, it turned out I had to banish the guards.
They were arming for a hostile takeover and . . .
hey! Hey! What are you doing?

Unpacking. The guards are gone.

No, you don't! Out of the living room. I've had
enough of you for one day. And take your family
with you! You've got way bigger jobs to do. Make
your way to the people who are sick and hungry,
to the ones fighting wars, the ones being tortured
and abused. My grief is petty in comparison. Out!

*Have it your way. But I'll be back. You can count on
that!*

I know. You are always hovering, waiting for that moment when the door opens and you can rush in.

Yep. And don't sell me short. I have many keys to that door: the smell of morning coffee, the red jacket still hanging in the closet, the morning surprise that the warm body you wake to is only a dog. So many keys to the door.

I can't keep you from visiting now and then, but you've got to keep these visits short. And next time, don't bring the whole family!

Being Old in the Pandemic

March 26, 2020, Day 62: 86 deaths, 4,062 known cases of the coronavirus in California

It is now two weeks since Governor Newsom urged people over the age of 65 to stay home. One week since he ordered all but essential workers to stay home.

At my kitchen table, sipping vinegar tea and nibbling a double fiber English muffin, I gaze out the front window on my quiet suburban street. That's how I start my days, at the table, alternately checking email and news on my laptop, glancing up to watch the neighborhood wake up. I keep scratch paper next to me in case there's something I want to remember from the news, or I happen to think of an item I need from the market, or anything else I want to remember. If I don't write it down when I think of it, it's often gone. At 85, the memory region of my brain is so damned full there's no real estate left where new memories can find a place to live. Today my scratch paper is an unopened envelope from AARP addressed to my husband, now six years dead.

I glance at the *NY Times* headlines. Anger rises in me as I see that Trump continues to refer to the virus as "the Chinese virus," and that anti-

Asian sentiment is growing. I think of my now grown, bright, beautiful, productive Chinese granddaughters and my outrage intensifies. The unreasonable stupidity of it all!

I shift my attention to emails. Before I get to anything I care about, I delete a message promising to make me rich, another needing my social security number in order to keep my bank account open, and countless pleas for political donations. I reply to a mildly amusing joke from a friend with a laughing emoji; answer another friend's request for a book recommendation; read highlights, or lowlights, of the news, and try to wrap my mind around the fact that the U.S. has more than 50,000 confirmed infections and 700 dead from the virus.

At 8:15 on a usual Tuesday morning there'd be a bunch of kids on their way to school—the older ones on bicycles, younger ones walk-skipping beside some adult, or pushing along ahead on one of those little scooter things. Those on bicycles would be wearing heavy backpacks draped across their young shoulders, their precious heads protected by helmets secured with chin straps. I wonder if they feel the same sense of freedom I had all of those decades ago, as I rode no-hands along a similar street, my hair blowing behind me. Unlike today's heavily-laden riders, all I had was a brown paper lunch bag that sat in the wire basket attached to the handlebars of my balloon-tired, red Schwinn. I sit straighter in my chair as my body re-senses that long ago ride, the slight shift of weight it took for me to make a wide hands-free turn at the corner.

Unlike a usual Tuesday morning though, this one is eerily quiet. Schools have been closed for a week now with no reopening date in sight. Children are not scooting along the sidewalks or zipping along on their bikes. Wherever possible, people are working from home. Cars are still parked in driveways or at the curb, none creeping carefully toward the corner stop sign, making the left turn to take them out of the neighborhood and on their way to work.

Sometime between 9:00-9:30, the neighborhood will awaken, but by that time I'll be away from my morning post, tidying up, or maybe searching for another piece to fit into the goddamned jigsaw puzzle—the puzzle I wish I'd never started. Jigsaw puzzles. They're all over the place these days, people trading them through Nextdoor or arranging for exchanges on the church website, which is how I got this one. I thought a 1,000-piece puzzle of Nancy Drew book covers would be easy—just focus on the book titles and the whole thing would fall in place. What I hadn't considered was how repetitious the titles would be—The Clue in the . . . The Secret at . . . The Mystery of . . . with the author's name, "Carolyn Keene," on every book cover. Then there's all that blonde hair! The puzzle now sits with the border filled in and the rest of the 840 pieces strewn about on the leaf-extended dining table, taunting me every time I walk past it.

After watering the potted plants in my little patio, I change shoes and start my morning walk. Supposedly, the magic number of daily steps leading to both good physical health and good brain health is 10,000. I generally log about half of that most days, apparently shooting for only mediocre physical and brain health.

Lately on my walks I've been seeing colorful sidewalk chalk drawings of rainbows, hearts, and more free-form designs. Several windows along the way have signs with mottos such as "We're All In This Together," and "Thank You, First Responders!" As I approach other walkers, one of us steps off the sidewalk to allow a distance of at least six feet between us. We smile, say "Hi." Although I've never thought of our neighborhood as unfriendly, the pandemic has brought with it a stronger sense of community and camaraderie.

By 1:00 I'm back at the table, not the puzzle table, the other table. I'm back with a tuna sandwich, apple, and iced tea, gazing out on the awakened neighborhood. Three girls, aged seven to nine is my guess, are riding bikes around the cul-de-sac, circling without destination. In the catty-corner yard, two boys who look to be about six are jammed into one of those saucer-like swings, the dad twisting it taut, giving the boys a fast spin when he lets go. Between the kids on my block and those on the adjacent cul-de-sac, there are somewhere between ten and fifteen kids under the age of twelve. I get a different number every time I count, probably because they move so fast, and also, they all sort of look alike.

From the outside, things look easy and smooth in my neighborhood, but I'm pretty sure it's not as idyllic as it looks from the window of my own orderly, quiet home. The idea of Mike and me sheltering in place for weeks with our three when they were school age is not reassuring.

What a different time this must be for families: mom and dad home all day, trying to work. Or maybe one or the other, or both of them, are essential workers, or there's a single parent—then what? And the kids all need supervision and motivation for online school work.

The abrupt transition from the school they know to an experiment in online education. The fear of infection. The isolation from grandparents who are more at risk—so many sudden life changes! I'm aware that this pandemic may be the first collective shared memory for them—the first awareness that the world beyond them directly affects their lives. Will this pandemic be to them what the bombing of Pearl Harbor and WWII were to my generation? That sudden realization that everything's changed now? Will they mark time by the Before, During, and After of the pandemic as my generation still marks time by the Before, During, and After of "The War"?

~

Just three months before the bombing of Pearl Harbor, I'd gone to San Pedro with my parents, grandmother, Aunt Alice and Uncle Tommy, to see my Aunt Hazel off to Honolulu on the *S. S. Lurline*. I was a big girl, almost six, wearing shiny black patent leather shoes that were hard to run in.

We wandered the ship with Auntie Hazel and found her stateroom. She was on her way to marry her high school sweetheart, Henry, who was in the Army Air Corps, stationed at Hickham Field. It was a happy, festive time. Everyone was dressed up: Granny in her church dress and hat, my mother and Aunt Alice also in hats and dressy dresses; my father and Uncle Tommy in suits and ties. When it was time, we all hugged Auntie Hazel goodbye and followed the crowd down the gangplank. Back on shore we waved wildly and my aunt waved back at us as the ship slowly inched away from the dock. We threw long paper streamers while the band played "Aloha Oe," then the ship sounded two long horn blasts and picked up speed.

A week or two after the sendoff, Granny got a framed picture of Uncle Henry in his uniform and Auntie Hazel in a long white dress, standing by two tall palm trees. Soon we were getting regular letters and Kodak pictures showing their cottage near the base, new friends, and the beach—the ocean reported to be "warm as bathwater."

Somewhere along the way I got a grass skirt and a lei but I don't remember if they were from Aunt Hazel and Uncle Henry, or some other lover of all things Hawaiian. The lei itched. Occasionally my mother looked longingly at the pictures and said how she always wished she could go to Hawaii. Sometimes she played a record of Bing Crosby singing "Blue Hawaii." I liked the other side of the record better: "Sweet Leilani." It is strange that I can't remember what I need at the market, but just the title of that song brings back a whole chunk of the lyrics, as sung by Bing Crosby. And now I'm remembering Harry Owens and his Royal Hawaiians, and Hilo Hattie.

I still remember clearly the news that Pearl Harbor had been bombed, my mother and grandmother sitting close on the couch, crying, my father pacing. I was six years old and had never before seen grownups cry. I'd never before heard the Japanese, people like the family who owned the produce section where my father had his meat market, referred to as "dirty Japs." I'd never known anyone who died, as my Uncle Henry did in the bombing, leaving Aunt Hazel a widow at the age of twenty.

There were a lot of Befores and Afters, and a wealth of Durings too. Before the war, when we could still get butter, when we could take a trip in the car, when horses still raced around the track at Santa Anita. During the war, when Santa Anita Racetrack was turned into an internment camp for Japanese families, and later, a prisoners of war camp. During the war, there were so many dads and brothers missing from home and moms going to work. There were paper drives, air raid practices, saving tinfoil and fat for the war effort, rationing because the boys overseas needed meat and cigarettes, butter and sugar, to keep going. Rationing gasoline was necessary to maintain an adequate supply for jeeps and truck convoys, planes and tanks in battle. Oil for explosives. Nylon for parachutes and flak jackets. Accepting and supporting rationing was our patriotic duty. We were all in it together.

After the war, Detroit went back to manufacturing cars rather than tanks. Nylons and cigarettes were readily available again, and we could throw away our ration books. After the war, instead of driving past orange groves and strawberry fields on our way to the beach, we drove past acres and acres of cookie-cutter tract houses for returning G.I.s and their just-starting families. My loyal native Californian mother claimed that once they'd seen California on their way to combat overseas, they didn't want to live anywhere else.

~

In the year 2102, when the neighborhood kids are all in their 80s, will they judge time by their Before, During, and After? Will the shift to online learning, the loss of a grandparent, the mask-wearing and constant handwashing remain firmly entrenched in their memory banks, crowding out the birthdate of their most recent great-grandchild? Will they have a sense of "we were all in it together," like our generation did, or will they remember dissension over mask-wearing, vaccinations, and shutdowns?

July 29, 2020, Day 185: 8,518 deaths, 466,550 reported cases of the coronavirus in California

It is a clear, bright day with a predicted high of 98. Sunlight beams through the corner windows of the bedroom I use as an office. A red-headed hummingbird hovers at the feeder just outside my window. Several of the free-range neighborhood kids zip along the sidewalk, followed by a little one who can barely reach the handlebars of his scooter. He is sucking a pacifier as he pushes hard to keep up. The pack leaders cut diagonally across the street to the house with two large saucer swings and a tree with a ladder of boards that make climbing up to the first branch easy. A woman walks past with a large dog on a leash and I watch to see if she's the one who doesn't clean up after her big dog leaves a mountain of shit on my front lawn. They walk past without a pause. She's carrying a plastic poop bag, but that may just be for show.

I check my bank balance, happy to see that my teacher's retirement check has been deposited. That's usually the case by the 29th, but not always. I go to "Bill Pay" and enter payments for the bills that are soon to be due. There aren't many. Rent, utilities, wi-fi, Netflix, phone, car payment, a credit card that I pay off every month. In the past, there may have been a Macy's charge, or J. Jill, but since there's no in-person shopping these days, the slots to enter payment beside these companies remain vacant. The pandemic is definitely a money-saving event.

Back in March we thought the shutdown might last a few weeks, maybe even a month. Now it seems there's no end in sight. I don't like the phrase "the new normal" that has recently become so common it's sliding into the realm of cliché, but I guess it expresses the truth about our present situation, like it or not. I'm now used to ordering groceries online and picking them up curbside, same with take-out food. I'm used to Zoom committee meetings, online writing groups, and Sunday morning Zoom church. Being on Zoom feels stiff to me and I sorely miss having personal contact. It is, though, to fall back on another phrase that has gained use these past months, "better than nothing."

It's been four months since anyone other than myself has been inside my house. Except for an overnight recovery period at the home of friends after I had a pacemaker installed, it's also been four months since I've been inside anyone else's house. Four months since I've sat at my friend's poker chip-laden table and participated in friendly banter about the purity of "Texas Hold 'Em" and the impurity of "No Peek" and "Follow the Queen" poker. It's been four months since I've experienced the lift of spirit that comes with being in church. Four months since I've driven the hundred or so miles for an overnight visit with my daughter and her family. I'm missing it all. It turns out I'm less of an introvert than I thought I was.

Later in the day, I walk a few blocks to a Little Free Library where I leave my just-finished copy of *White Fragility*. It's a small thing, this sending books that address social and racial justice out into the world. Because of Covid I'm not out there marching with Black Lives Matter, but spreading the word through books is something I *can* do.

I say this as if there's no question that I'd be out there marching for racial justice if not for Covid. Would I? I like to think I would. I marched for Black Lives Matter a few years ago, protesting the police killing of Stephon Clark, a local Black man. In the more distant past, I marched for civil rights and women's rights, against the war in Vietnam and inhumane anti-immigration policies. The truth, though, is that I often don't rise to the occasion, choosing instead to bemoan the state of affairs from the comfort of my own living room. But back to books.

Since the brutal killing of George Floyd back in May, I've been leaving books by Black authors: Maya Angelou, James Baldwin, Toni Morrison.

Alice Walker, Bryan Stevenson, and Young Adult authors Jason Reynolds, Sharon Draper, Angie Thomas, in various Little Free Libraries throughout and beyond my neighborhood. These have mostly been fiction and autobiographies from my personal collection: books I've been holding onto because they meant something to me. They offered new insights into the lives of others and allowed me to see the world through other eyes. A few books I purchased specifically to spread around: Bryan Stevenson's *Just Mercy,* and Angie Thomas's *The Hate U Give,* four copies each. I'll probably never know if any of this makes a difference. What I *do* know, both from my own reading experiences and decades of teaching experience, is that books have the power to change lives.

~

I make a pitcher of iced tea, then fill the squirrel-proof patio bird feeder with hulled sunflower seeds, which the little finches love, top off the other hanging bird feeder with a wild bird seed mix, which they love less. I move yesterday's wet clothes from the washer to the dryer and start the "energy preferred" cycle. Sometime tomorrow I'll fold the dried laundry and put it away, all the while berating myself for turning a task that requires less than an hour of active work into a three-day chore. Oh, well. Such is life.

"Such is life?" Where the hell did that long forgotten phrase come from? It arrives in my mother's resigned tone of voice, followed by her martyrish sigh. "A blast from the past"—as long as I'm sinking into the clichés of the fifties. Truly from the fifties? I add "such is life" and "blast from the past" to my list of things to Google. I've spent most of my life not being my mother; too often working on *not* being, rather than being. Still she manages to push through the barrier of my subconscious with a phrase, an unwelcome attitude, the scent of Jean Naté . . . Never mind. It's time to get out of my head and into someone else's. I open the Audible app on my iPhone, check to see that my hearing aids are connected to Bluetooth, and go to *A Promised Land*. It's good to get Barack Obama's voice into my head for a while. I love hearing his steady calm, his reasoned intellect. Even better than getting my own voice out of my head, he blocks out that other lying, bombastic fool's voice for a while.

May 17, 2021, Day 479: 61,510 deaths, 3,665,904 cases of the coronavirus in California

This past Thursday, the Centers for Disease Control and Prevention announced a major relaxation of face mask guidelines, suggesting that fully vaccinated people can stop wearing masks in most places, either outdoors or inside. Dr. Rochelle Walensky, CDC director, stated that "Anyone who is fully vaccinated can participate in indoor and outdoor activities, large or small, without wearing a mask or physical distancing." Unvaccinated or partly vaccinated people should still wear masks as should those using any form of public transportation.

Fast forward to May 24. Mornings at 8:00, the kids are again out on bicycles and scooters, sporting backpacks and helmets, zipping their way toward school. The "We're In It Together" window signs and heart chalk drawings have long faded from sight. Still, there seems to be a stronger sense of community than in pre-Covid days. I know more of my neighbors by name. More of my neighbors know me.

When I walk at dusk, I often see groups of three to ten people in a circle of chairs on a front lawn. These are not the pair of Adirondack chairs that sit empty on lawns or porches, serving only decorative purposes. These are outdoor patio-style chairs, folding chairs, soccer mom chairs, chairs meant for sitting. I think, I hope, this will be a lasting benefit of the shutdown: ongoing socializing on our front lawns. I'll do my part by inviting a few to my own lawn for a BYOB cocktail hour later this week.

On Thursday, safely boosted, I had my first meal inside a restaurant in over a year. I walked in masked, then removed it once I was seated. What a treat it was, ordering from a menu, being served. I liked it so much I ate out again on Saturday and Sunday.

In June, there'll be a big family get-together at Stinson Beach, a celebration for my son-in-law's 65th (!) birthday. We will all have been vaccinated by then, so both our inside and outside gatherings can be mask-free. In July, I'll fly to Walla Walla to visit my son and his family. My niece from Kansas City is coming for a visit in September. I'm something of an introvert so I didn't think the Covid-related confinement had much effect on me, but the easing of restrictions has left me feeling lighter, freer. It's similar to how I felt after Trump finally left the White House. It was as if a heavy burden had been lifted from my shoulders. There's room for optimism, and optimism is a great gift for anyone in their eighties and beyond. I welcome the gift.

Pronoun Practice

I'm trying to catch up, to change my lifelong expectation that "their" and "they" mean more than one. I'm trying to learn this new language. I got "LGB" decades ago. And the trans "T" was an easy add-on. So was "Q." I caught up with that before most of my contemporaries, half of whom are dead now. I miss them. Some of them. Someday people will be missing me, too, some of them, though so far it looks as if it's going to have to be younger people who miss me.

I'll celebrate my 86th birthday next month. I'll want all 86 candles on my cake in order to show off that I can still blow them all out, not like my younger cousin, who is on oxygen, nor like my longtime friend who can no longer tell a candle from a light bulb. Not like another good friend who stopped breathing decades ago.

Anyway, LGBTQ was easy. But this? A young woman . . . Not a woman! I've got to stop calling her a woman. Stop calling them a woman? Awkward.

One evening at church last week, a young *person* proudly announced that she—not *she*, this *person*—announced that ~~she~~ *the person* was nonbinary. ~~She'd~~ They'd changed ~~her~~ their name from Margaret to Pat and ~~her~~ their preferred pronouns are now "they" and "them." Pat is going, alone, to the market where *they* will buy a loaf of bread. My old Arkansas aunt would have declared, "Oooooeeee, that just don't sound *right*. God ain't gonna like that."

That traditionally plural pronoun used for one person doesn't sound right to me either, but I'm not my old Arkansas aunt. I'm happy that people are free to identify themselves however they want to. That's a good thing. It's just hard to use that common plural noun for a single person. I told Margaret-turned-Pat that Pat was easy. That the non-binary idea was easy. Pretty easy. But "they" and "them" would be a challenge for me.

"They is going to take their clothes to the Laundromat?" I don't think so.

She'd asked . . . No, not "she." Pat. Pat asked, "Do you have a pet?"

"Lily, my dog."

"Practice pronouns on your dog. They won't mind."

~

I like the concept of gender fluidity, the concept that people are free to live according to their self-perception. This concept was not widely held, or maybe even considered by the general public, when I could have benefited from such acceptance back in the late thirties-early forties. If I could have lived as a boy back then, I'd have done it. Boys had more fun. I knew that truth from the time I was five. Christmas. Richard Metz, across the street, got an electric train that chugged around his whole living room, going through tunnels, belching out steam, and choo-chooing all the way. Richard Metz got an electric train and I got a damned Betsy Wetsy doll! Why would I want to change the damned diapers on a damned doll?

From five until around thirteen when the damned girlie hormones kicked in, I wanted to be a boy. I didn't have penis envy but I did have boy envy. I wanted clothes that were more adaptable to tree climbing than dresses were. Clothes that didn't demand that I keep my legs together, clothes that when hanging upside down on the playground bars didn't elicit, "I see London! I see France! I see Marilyn's underpants!"

Besides the practicality and comfort of boys' clothes, there was the more amorphous desire to dress like my daddy and my cousin Jim and to *be* like them when I grew up. It was obvious to me that my daddy and Jim and their friends laughed a lot more than my mother and *her* friends. They told funny stories about some ol' boy down on the farm who lost his false teeth while fishing on Cameron's pond, or a persnickety customer at Daddy's market who wanted to smell the fish before she bought it, and they laughed full out. They played poker and drank beer, and smoked, and laughed their rolling laughter.

With my mother and her friends, there was laughter, but to my child's ears their laughter seemed tight and restricted. And often their voices would whine about some slight from a husband or neighbor. And there was the tight-faced worry about money, or a child, or a sick relative. No wonder I wanted to be a boy, grow up to be a man.

When I and the neighborhood boys dug fox holes in the back yard playing army, I refused to be a WAC. I was an army sergeant! I shot more Germans than anyone.

Nearly all of the photos of me during that time show me sitting or standing stiffly in a fancy dress, with black patent-leather Mary Janes and a giant bow in my hair. A few show me in shorts or a bathing suit but those were all at the beach. There is, however, one photo of me in slacks, probably around nine years-old, taken in front of our house. They're not play-clothes slacks but nice slacks, with suspenders over a shirt with a collar. My hair is parted neatly in the middle and pulled back into two braids. There is no bow. I don't look stiff.

According to my good friend Ms. Google, slacks became more acceptable as women's wear in the 1930s and '40s. Both Marlene Dietrich and Katharine Hepburn famously wore slacks, so I guess that moved the practice forward. I don't recall ever seeing my mother in slacks but her younger sister, my Aunt Hazel, often wore slacks.

I remember negotiating with my mother to wear slacks to school, in first or second grade, I think. Although it was unusual for girls to wear slacks back then, I don't think there were any rules against it. And, if memory serves (always questionable), we did reach an agreement that I could wear slacks to school once a week.

On the school playground I wanted to play real basketball, like the boys, not that damned boring one-bounce, no-dribbling basketball the girls were supposed to play. I wanted the freedom of pants and a jersey shirt, not the restrictions that went with behaving properly in girls' clothes. Watching the women basketball players in the Tokyo Olympics, it's obvious that these women were not confined by the one-bounce rule when they were growing up.

If I could have been gender fluid back then, I would definitely have chosen maleness. Upon reflection, though, I realize that it was not maleness that I desired so much as the freedom that went with it.

Hanging in my closet today are sixteen pairs of pants, nine tailored shirts, eight long, loose-fitting sweaters (yes, it's time for another thrift store donation!). Crowded together at one end are three seldom worn skirts and two even less often worn dresses. On the shelf over the hanging clothes are two pair of worn jeans, a stack of folded sweatshirts and another stack of long-sleeved turtleneck tee-shirts.

Am I living as a man? Nah. I do, though, enjoy the freedom to dress in clothing that would allow for tree-climbing, if I were to decide to climb a tree. At this stage of my life I'm happy to live with my birth-given gender. That said, I'm all for gender fluidity, and finding a vocabulary for those who choose to be neither "he" nor "she," but I'm afraid that "their" and "they" used as singular pronouns will always elicit a fingernails-on-chalkboard cringe. But I'll work on it.

Lily stirs from where ~~she's~~ they've been sleeping by my feet, rises, stretches, and scratches at my leg. They probably need to go outside. Soon it will be time to feed them.

How'm I doing?

Give a Little Whistle

When I open the front door for my friend to leave, my miniature poodle, Lily, zips out to the sidewalk where she then sits facing me. I don't know if she's truly a miniature poodle. She has a checkered past and is of unknown descent.

The one thing I have managed to teach her is to come when called. After a myriad of practices with high-value treats, she unfailingly comes running to me, top speed, from wherever, whenever I call her. Unfailingly, that is, until today. Today she sits unmoving on the sidewalk, looking at me.

"Lily, come!" I call again.

She sits still as a statue, watching.

"LILY, COME!" I repeat and repeat. She sits and sits.

My friend, Anara, standing on the front porch witnessing the rebellion, purses her lips and whistles. Lily comes running! She stops before me and sits in the "I-expect-my-treat-now" position. I don't think so, Lily.

I add "tasty treats" to my grocery list with a plan to give Lily some intense remedial "come" training. I'm puzzled that she came so quickly to Anara's whistle. It wasn't even a loud, fingers-in-the-mouth whistle, just a pursed lips whistle. Was that a leftover response from a previous owner? Seems unlikely. A Sacramento rescue group had snatched Lily from the jaws of death at a kill facility in Merced. She was extremely malnourished and fearful, and spent six weeks in a foster home being acclimatized to kindness and healthy living before she was available for adoption. Except with children, she's still skittish around others, both people and dogs. There were three kids where she was fostered. Maybe they taught her to come to a whistle?

Later in the day I decide to experiment. Lily is at her usual post in front of the kitchen slider, looking out on the patio. I'm in my office. I lick my lips, purse, and blow. There is only the slightest sound of exhaled breath. I try again. Nothing. What??? I've been able to whistle since I was four years old and now I can't whistle? Is whistling one of those skills old people lose, like turning cartwheels and remembering phone numbers?

I never did learn that two-fingered, ear-piercing whistle that the across-the-street neighbor used to call her kids in at dinnertime, but I could whistle to get someone's attention. I could whistle a tune! I try to think back to the last time I whistled. Nothing comes to mind. I again purse my lips and blow. Still no sound.

Except for Anara, I also can't remember the last time I even heard someone whistle. It gets me wondering if the practice of whistling has fallen by the wayside, like burning trash, or taking pictures with a camera. It seemed everyone whistled when I was growing up in that little town of

Temple City in Southern California. My father whistled a low tune while he sliced lunchmeat, or ground hamburger, or swept the sawdust in his meat market. My cousin Jim whistled on his morning walk to work in that same market. I don't think I ever heard my granny whistle. Maybe she couldn't whistle with false teeth.

The best whistler I ever knew was Dorothy, of Dorothy and Nardi, our neighbors on Cloverly Street. They had just moved into a newly built house next door to ours and, for reasons long lost to me, I was in the kitchen watching Dorothy line the cupboard shelves. She was sitting on the floor, whistling, cutting paper to size, then sliding it into a low cupboard shelf. I was standing eye level with the top of the cupboard door. Maybe I was four. I remember being impressed with Dorothy's whistling. She was whistling a popular song, one I liked, maybe "Three Little Fishies" or "Jeepers Creepers." I was impressed that the sound was full and pure, melodic, though I wouldn't have described it in those terms then. I just thought she was a really good whistler.

Maybe the person lining shelves today is listening to a podcast. Maybe someone on the way to work is talking on a cell phone. I wonder if it's still a great accomplishment if a kid learns to whistle? Although no longer a kid, my 26-year-old granddaughter, Subei, is definitely closer to kiddom than anyone else I know. When we meet for lunch a few days after Lily's rush to a whistle, I ask if she remembers when she first learned to whistle. Was it a big deal? She smiles at the memory.

"Totally! When I learned to whistle and also to snap my fingers!"

"How old were you?"

"Four, I think. Maybe five? Those were important markers to me back then. I was on my way to becoming a big girl," she says with a laugh.

"Do you ever hear friends, or anyone, whistling? Maybe while they're involved in a task, or just walking along? Anyone whistling a tune?"

She shakes her head. The only whistling she might hear is that loud two-fingered whistle at a sporting event, or to call an unleashed dog back. I mention whistling contests, wondering if they're still as big a deal as ever. Subei does a couple of quick swipes on her ever-present phone.

"Oh, wow," she says, "they're all over—national, international; popular, classical; accompanied, non-accompanied . . ."

The waitress comes with the dessert menu and our conversation naturally turns from whistling to chocolate cheesecake and ice cream sundaes.

On the way home, in the privacy of my car, I experiment with blowing air through various mouth/tongue positions. I'm determined to get my whistle back but so far, no luck.

At home I look to YouTube for whistling help. You can learn anything on YouTube. Just last week YouTube taught me how to unplug my toilet without using a plunger; surely it can help me regain my whistle.

I've made my peace with never again doing a cartwheel, or standing on my head, or even getting up from the floor without first awkwardly turning to a hands and knees crawling position and bumbling myself upward. But I'm not willing to never whistle again, goddamn it!

Sure enough, several possibilities come up on YouTube—tutorials on how to whistle loudly, with fingers, without fingers, etc. I choose "How to whistle in 3 EASY Steps!" First there's an ad for "Mandalorian," reminding me that Disney has moved far beyond Bambi. Then there's loud, grating music, not whistling, accompanying the name of the whistle teacher in large, three dimensional letters. Let's call him LARRY O for the sake of anonymity. He starts out with "What's up guys?" which reminds me that this is not a video directed at my demographic. Then he proceeds to talk so fast I can barely understand him. Then, while he's telling us that several people, some of them *actual* friends, have been begging him to make such a video, a message flashes on the screen saying "Let's try to reach 40 likes guys!"

I'm already so irritated by LARRY O's talking at top speed and addressing me as a guy, I'm ready to switch to the "Whistling Tutorial (without fingers)." But as annoying as this "guy" is, he at least knows how to use an apostrophe, so I'll give him another minute. LARRY O's first tip is to say the word "two" and leave your lips in that position, the right spot for whistling. I do that. Next, position your tongue against your bottom teeth. "Yike iss," he says, trying to demonstrate the position and talk at the same time. Then he says to cave your tongue in the middle and leave the sides higher. My tongue won't cave in the middle so I skip to the last step—blow lightly. Yes!! There's a sound! Probably not enough to call Lily with, but a step in the right direction!

I decide LARRY O's not so bad after all. His fast-talking, nervous hair-touching gestures, the pimple on his forehead, and his video's bland beige background in what is probably his childhood bedroom, all elicit a sort of motherly empathy—or, more age appropriately, great-grandmotherly empathy. I make another whistle sound, this time with two tones. Faint, but still . . . I'm so happy that I leave a thumbs up. I don't, though, succumb to Larry's pitch to subscribe to his videos. He's already taught me what I need to know.

In the week that follows, I practice whistling when I'm alone in the car, or when Lily's with Roger. I want to wait until my whistle is strong before she hears it but I've now got a pretty good "Jingle Bells."

In addition to practicing my whistle, the subject of whistling keeps pushing up through my subconscious to demand attention. The phrase "clean as a whistle" jumps to mind as I wipe down the kitchen counter. The seven dwarfs march across my consciousness singing and whistling their familiar rendition of "Whistle While You Work." I'm thinking about a whistleblower in the news recently who exposed the horrendous conditions children were living in at ICE facilities at the U.S.-Mexico border.

And then the old scary radio program, "The Whistler" comes to mind. I turn to Ms. Google, who plays the opening tune from a 1946 broadcast. There is the creaking door, the spooky whistled tune that ends with a harsh minor chord, the voice of the mysterious Whistler who knows "the many secrets hidden in the hearts of men and women" and "the nameless terrors of which they dare not speak." The immediate familiarity catapults me back to my childhood bedroom. I am ten years old, lying in my single bed, a twin to the one across the room that is sometimes used for a sleepover friend or a visiting relative. On this night it is only me in the bedroom. The covers are pulled tight against my chin. The room is dark except for the faint glow from the dial of my ivory Bakelite Hoffman radio. The volume is set low in hopes that my forbidden afterhours radio listening will escape notice.

The voice, the footsteps, a light, steady rain with distant thunder, the eerie whistling, all fill me with foreboding before I've even been introduced to the sinister story. I am back there in that bedroom, with that radio, that streetlight at that curb casting the dimmest of light through Venetian blinds at the window.

I mustn't let the past outweigh the present so I leave "The Whistler" and my childhood bedroom, and turn to that place we're all advised to live, "in the now." I water the parched patio plants. I bring in hydrangea blossoms to brighten the mantle. I read new email. Later, while Lily is outside, napping in her favorite patio chair, I stand just inside the door, lick my lips, purse them in the "two" position, and blow out an acceptably strong whistle. Lily rouses! She runs through the dog door and sits at my feet in treat position! I shower her with treats and praise. Several times over the course of the day I whistle for her. Several times she comes. I'm as pleased with myself over this revived skill as I was a few weeks ago when I finished my 1,000-piece jigsaw puzzle depicting Nancy Drew book covers. Maybe the key to happiness at 85 is meeting a simple, self-set challenge. I'm not sure what's next—maybe perfecting the finger snap. Or maybe honing my whistling skill to reproduce The Whistler's theme song. It won't be cartwheels.

Wondering

I find myself wondering about things, sometimes talking about things, that are of little or no interest to the people around me. Covering the half-eaten dinner of Trader Joe's Palak Paneer with aluminum foil, I wonder: when did aluminum foil come into common usage? My mother used waxed paper to cover food or wrap sandwiches. I remember the roll of waxed paper that sat lengthwise in the bread drawer, beside the ever-present loaf of white Weber's Bread. I think it was in a blue and white package, but that may have been Wonder Bread. Our family had a brand loyalty to Weber's Bread. We didn't eat Wonder Bread. We drank Cokes, not Pepsi, and my father smoked Camels, not Lucky Strike. But aluminum foil? Was there also a roll of aluminum foil next to the waxed paper? I don't think so.

In the bottom drawer under *my* sink counter are waxed paper, aluminum foil, Saran Wrap, parchment paper, and two containers of plastic baggies, one sandwich-sized and one larger, large enough to contain ample Cheerios to feed two toddlers if I were of a mind to go searching for toddlers to whom I could feed Cheerios.

My childhood family didn't eat General Mills Cheerios. We ate Kellogg's Pep. Not Wheaties. There is no bread in the current bottom drawer, the one that contains rolls of materials with which one can cover or wrap food, or cook on, or add to the accumulation of clutter that now threatens the earth and seas. There is no bread in that drawer because: too many carbs. Growing up, carbohydrates made up the bulk of our food pyramid, but the word "carbohydrates" was not part of the family vocabulary.

According to Ms. Google, aluminum foil supplanted tin foil in the mid-20th century. Tin foil! I'd forgotten all about tin foil. Balls of tin foil growing larger with each stick of gum we chewed, until we turned them in somewhere. Where? Where was it that we donated our tin foil balls so we could beat Hitler and Tojo?

Ms. Google says that the first formed, all-foil food containers appeared on the market in 1948, with a folded, cook-in design. This grew into the complete line of die-formed and air-formed foil containers now sold in every grocery store and supermarket, either as product-containing packages, or as convenience dishes and pans. In 1949, large-scale promotion and distribution of institutional foil quickly expanded.

In 1949, I would have been fourteen. My mother would have been thirty-eight. Less than half my age right now. I try to picture the thirty-eight year old Esther with her first roll of aluminum foil. Was the first covering of leftovers with foil a thrilling event? On her daily phone conversation with my fake-Aunt Ethel, who was really my mother's *double* cousin, did they talk about the new-found conveniences of aluminum foil? It may not have been quite the miracle that Tupperware was. There were Tupperware parties, but I don't think there were ever aluminum foil parties. When did Tupperware come into use? One more conversation to save for Ms. Google. She may not be any more interested in my meandering thoughts than the living, breathing people around me, but at least her eyes don't glaze over.

"Eyes glaze over." I've never really liked that phrase. When did that come into common usage, anyway? Before aluminum foil? After Saran Wrap? I'm going to stop this right now. I'm going to stop and go to the market, buy a loaf of Weber's Bread, come home and smear both slices of the bread with butter, pour a thick layer of ketchup (not catsup, ketchup) on top of one buttered slice of bread, top it with the other buttered slice. Cut off the crusts, cut the sandwich in half. Horizontally (never diagonally), to make a perfect replica of the sandwich I ate for lunch, every day, at South Santa Anita School. I'll eat that sandwich as if it were 1942, except instead of washing it down with a Coke, maybe I'll wash it down with a couple of glasses of Chardonnay.

I like being old, following my thoughts wherever they take me, washing my ketchup sandwich down with whatever the hell pleases me.

Remember Me?

I'm two months away from eighty-six and, although I'm physically healthy and (mostly) cognitively intact, at random times a little man with a picket sign marches through my consciousness shouting, "The end is near! The end is near!" forcing me to consider what crucial information is missing from my "Final Exit" portable file box.

The will is there, handwritten per instructions found online and checked free of charge by an attorney located through the local senior center. It's simple. Everything (which sounds like more than it is) is divided equally among my three children. My brother, nine years younger than I, whose end is likely not quite so near and who everyone trusts, is the executor.

My son is named as my literary executor, which also sounds like more than it is.

There's my birth certificate. There's Mike's birth certificate, death certificate, and our wedding license, which sound like less than they are. There's the pink slip to the Prius, along with repair records, and the necessary paperwork from the Nautilus Cremation Society, which sounds exactly like what it is.

As for how I want to be remembered, my fear is that my life will be reduced to a few simplistic impressions like we've always done with Aunt

Gladys—remember how she'd be drinking all night, perfectly fine, then suddenly be totally drunk in the middle of the sentence? Or like we've done with our mother, quoting and re-quoting her assessment of every movie we ever took her to see: "Well, it was pretty impossible, but they took their parts well." But if I don't want to be reduced to an ongoing bad habit, or a few trite remarks, I'd better put in writing what I *do* want to be remembered for and slam it into the Final Exit file. But first, what about the music?

Lately, at church on Sundays, with each hymn or musical offering, I'm wondering, do I want this at my going away party? These are Unitarian Universalist hymns, not the rousing Baptist hymns I grew up with. I love "I'll Fly Away, Oh Glory," but I don't want the party revelers thinking I believed that baloney. "There is a Fountain Filled with Blood" might be good if I somehow end up bleeding to death, but that's unpredictable.

It could be something secular, like that song we were so fond of in high school, "Roll Me Over in the Clover." Not all of the verses would be appropriate but maybe "This is number seven and I'm on my way to heaven . . ." would be okay—still not theologically sound, though.

One of my favorite UU hymns starts, "Spirit of life, come unto me . . ." but it will be too late for that. How about "So Long It's Been Good to Know You?" Better. I'll look through my "Sing Along with Mitch Miller" collection. That has possibilities.

But back to what I'll be remembered for? If this bit of writing is any indication, I'll probably be remembered for not sticking to the subject.

Time Travels to the Clock Broiler

With so much material available to revisit, my old brain time-travels, place-travels, people-travels, through long dormant memories. Often there's no apparent reason why, while sitting at my iMac, being a part of the modern world doing my online banking, I'm suddenly also at my Aunt Ruth's oilcloth-covered table in her McNeil, Arkansas, kitchen. We're drinking sweet tea, because in Arkansas in 1948, it's as if there's a law against making iced tea without sugar.

Or how, as I'm practicing mindfulness on my daily walk, my mind jumps to my father's meat market, where I am dangling like a side of beef, clutching the cold metal hook of the ceiling scale, while my father checks my weight, then, with his greasy pencil, writes the results on the wall, at the bottom of a row of earlier dates and weights, next to phone numbers for fat renderers, bookies, and packing houses.

Today though, I know exactly what catapults me back to the Clock Broiler, Temple City, California, 1952. It is a poem that showed up in my email inbox this morning, courtesy of "The Writer's Almanac." The author is Barbara Crooker, and the title is "Patty's Charcoal Drive-In." It is the poet's mention of silver trays hooked to car windows, "the mingled smells of seared meat patties, salty ketchup, rich sweet malteds," that presses my internal time-travel switch.

I am at the Clock, seventeen years old, my little brother in the back seat of my '47 Chevy, Bobbi Ruggles in the passenger seat. It's Saturday and our boyfriends are working at Howie's Market in San Gabriel, so we won't be hanging out with them until after 7:00. And my mother is working at my father's market in Temple City, so I'm stuck taking care of eight-year-old Dale.

Sometimes Bobbie and I like to eat inside, where it's easier to stay and talk longer. But we always have to go to the Drive-In when Dale is with us because he demands a cigarette whenever we light up. People inside the Clock give us mean looks if we let him smoke, and if we don't let him smoke with us, he starts crying and yelling, "I want a cigarette. Why won't you let me have a cigarette!" So the Drive-in just saves us a lot of trouble.

The car hop skates up to my window, order pad in hand. She's wearing a white blouse and red shorts. Or was that Twoheys in Alhambra where they wore white blouses and red shorts? I'm not really sure what the outfit was, but I know what we ordered: three cheeseburgers. God, I can taste those cheeseburgers right now! Three cheeseburgers, three orders of fries, two cokes for me and Dale, and a chocolate malted for Bobbie. We didn't have to order extra ketchup because those irritatingly small plastic envelope things that hold ketchup and mustard at fast food places hadn't yet been invented. An entire bottle of ketchup automatically came with our order at the Clock.

The good thing about being stuck with Dale on Saturdays, the *one* good thing, was that our mother gave us money for lunch, and a little extra for gas. She didn't give us money for cigarettes because she didn't know we smoked, and if she *had* known, she certainly wouldn't have supported our habit.

Earlier on, when tattletale Dale first saw us smoking it was, "I'm gonna tell Mom! You're not supposed to be smoking!"

"Want a cigarette?" I'd asked him.

Dale had long been fascinated with cigarettes, had walked around (practically since he could walk) with those fake cigarettes made from some disgusting chalk-like white candy. The size of a Pall Mall, it had a red tip on the end which was supposed to look like the glowing end of a real lit cigarette. Even at two or three, Dale constantly walked around with a pretend cigarette held between index and middle finger, tapping off pretend ashes after every pretend inhale. So he jumped at the chance for the real thing. I lit a Pall Mall and handed it to him. And it turned out he liked it.

"Mom'll be *really* mad if she finds out *you're* smoking because you're so much younger!"

The secret smoking practice was effective with Dale until 4th grade when the spoilsports at Longden Avenue School showed one of those preachy school movies about how smoking damages your lungs, and Dale, prone to hypochondria anyway, quit smoking right then and there. That night, at the dinner table, he announced to our parents, "Marilyn smokes all the time and everybody knows it but you."

Within a few days, though, I had my revenge. I'd learned of the power of suggestion, and every night before dinner I'd tell Dale privately that he was going to laugh when he ate his potatoes. (We *always* had potatoes at dinner.) He was going to laugh and he wouldn't be able to stop laughing.

The first night of my planted suggestion, Dale ate his pear and cottage cheese salad. He ate the pot roast. He ate the string beans. Then he sat looking at his potatoes.

"Eat your potatoes, Dale," my mother said.

"Yeah. Eat your potatoes," I told him.

He sat holding his fork, looking at the potatoes.

"You like mashed potatoes," my mother said. "Eat your potatoes."

Finally, he slowly, cautiously, slipped a halfbite of potatoes onto his fork. He slowly, cautiously raised the fork to his mouth, and then . . . he doubled up in laughter.

"Dale . . ." my father said, in that tone of voice that said more than we liked to hear.

Dale laughed harder and harder, gasping for breath. He was sent from the table, not to come back until he could behave as one should at the dinner table.

"I don't know what's wrong with that boy," my father said, shaking his head.

"Me either," I said, as I finished my last bite of potato.

After dinner I drove to Bobbie's, where we sat in my car and smoked our after-dinner cigarettes, and laughed about my payback to Dale. We talked about Tom and Pete, the boys we would go with later that evening to the Pioneer drive-in. The boys we would ultimately (and foolishly) marry, and ultimately (and wisely) divorce. But that was long after the Clock Drive-in had become a filling station, and Twoheys had closed the drive-in section of their restaurant, and the Pioneer was bulldozed to make room for road improvements.

I finally quit smoking after watching my three-year old daughter walk around with too many of those same chalk-like white, red-tipped candy cigarettes, watching her hold each one between index and middle finger, watching her tap off pretend ashes after every pretend inhale.

There was a time when I hardly knew anyone of age who didn't smoke. Today I know no one, personally, who is a regular smoker. On my neighborhood walks I do occasionally see a flattened cigarette butt, though the smoker is unknown to

me. It's been fifty-eight years since my last cigarette. I don't want to be in a room where people
are smoking. I'm happy that smoking is outlawed
in restaurants. It's been decades since I've owned
an ashtray.

A few months ago when one of my daughters
was helping me prepare for a yard sale, she retrieved from a storage box a "silent butler": a
round container, about 5" in diameter, silver-
plated with a hinged cover and a wooden handle.
I explained that it was used to collect ashes. She
looked at me blankly.

"You know. You've got company. Everyone's
smoking. Ashtrays fill up. Instead of taking them
to the kitchen trash to dump them you can just go
around with your silent butler and empty ashes
into that."

I didn't even have to look at her to see the
disbelief on her face.

Polishing the silver-plated silent butler puts
me in mind of other accessories of that earlier
time. There were cigarette cases and holders,
pocket lighters and table lighters. In my first marriage, one of our favorite wedding gifts was from
Dale: a beautiful marble Ronson table lighter and
matching cigarette holder set complete with an
oval silver-plated tray on which they sat in a place
of honor on the living room coffee table. Unlike
the silent butler, the Ronson set is long gone. I
have no idea what became of it. Maybe my first

husband took it with him when we split up, but I doubt it.

It's a good thing so few of us smoke these days—such a stinky, unhealthy habit. But sometimes, on a balmy Sacramento evening, on my patio, catching a light delta breeze during a lonely cocktail hour, I remember the comfort of the long draw on a filtered Winston, the leisurely exhale. I remember the feel of the cigarette between the index and middle finger of my right hand, the brief employment of the thumb to enable a flick of the ash. And I can picture myself in my patio glider, slowly sipping my vodka tonic, cigarette in hand, smoking in the style of Anne Bancroft in "The Graduate," or maybe Bette Davis in "All About Eve." At my age, I'm not worried about smoking pushing me to an early grave. If only it didn't taste so bad, smell so bad, make me want to puke. But wait a minute . . . what about vaping?? Wouldn't that offer the same benefits? Besides, it's never too late to develop a bad habit.

Spectator Shoes

Whatever happened to spectator shoes? Brown and white pumps, "two-tones" with a practical 2 ½" heel, not too high to walk the honeymoon hills of San Francisco in, steadied by the hand of my first husband. The worst husband. Shoes that went perfectly with the buff shantung going-away suit. The suit that I donned in the bedroom of my childhood, leaving the white wedding dress strewn across the bed for my mother to care for the next day.

It was a happy day, the day that I and my high school sweetheart promised "'til death do us part" in the little Baptist church with the picture of the white Jesus beaming down on us. It *was* a happy day. I can say that now. Probably one of the many happiest days in my 80-plus years of days. Just because that first marriage didn't end well, had worn out before the spectator shoes did, doesn't negate that gift of happiness.

We had a mostly good three years. Bought a house. Had two babies. I occasionally slipped on the spectator shoes and the shantung suit for an evening of dancing at the Pasadena Civic Auditorium. At midnight, as he held me close and we slow danced to "Good Night Ladies," I melted, just as I had in high school, at the combined scent of his Yardley's aftershave, the starched collar of his white dress shirt, the smoky residue of his Lucky Strikes.

Gradually though, his occasional weekend of overindulgence morphed into a daily drinking habit. Along with the daily drinking came random angry outbursts—slamming his fist so hard into the hood of the battery-dead car that he broke his hand, hurling a glass at the wall when he was bluffed out of a poker win, ripping cupboard doors open, then banging them shut because we were out of BBQ sauce. I lost respect for the man of my earlier dreams and with that, I lost love. I realized that I and our two young daughters would be better off without him, and I cut the ties.

For decades I only allowed myself to remember the drunken, angry aspects of my first husband. It was as if to honor that early happiness would be a betrayal of other later happinesses. Now, though, I sometimes find myself remembering back to those long ago times, the tender removal of a spectator shoe, the warmth of his hand on my calf as I sat on the edge of the honeymoon suite bed at the Pioneer Motel in Monrovia, California. The following days in the magical city, the love-filled nights in the St. Francis Hotel room.

I will never again walk the hills of San Francisco in spectator shoes, or feel the heat of young love, but I now know I can enjoy the memory of those early happy days of my life without diminishing later moments of happiness, or without discounting the love that lasted. Without lessening the present pleasure of walking city streets in comfortable orthotics, I can revel in the muscle memory of my feet slipping into those narrow-toed spectator shoes once more.

Non-Romantic Affairs of the Heart

Saturday, May 23, 2020. Covid cases, California: 90,631, Deaths: 3,708.

Since the Silver Sneakers exercise class shut down in March, I've been moving less and less. At first, I was determined to walk at least three miles most days in the neighborhood and do some regular weight lifting and stretching at home. It's amazing to me that after so many decades of body care promises made (and quickly broken), I can still spend hours of head-time confidently, and uselessly, making physical improvement plans. If I were married to someone who lied to me as often as I do, I'd get a divorce. But oh no, here we are: me and me, still together, living with lies.

On this day, noon-ish, I'm berating myself because I have been so lazy that I've only taken my neighborhood walk a couple of times, and then only around the block. I vow to turn over yet another new leaf, don my walking shoes and sun visor, and start down Minerva on the shady side of the street. I'm exhausted after less than a block. This is beyond lazy. As I drag my way back home, I take an inventory of symptoms. No fever, chills, cough, shortness of breath, nausea, or sore throat—just worn out. Probably not the corona-virus.

I think back over the past week or two. An occasional afternoon napper, naps have recently become a daily habit. I always used to set the timer for 45 minutes, but lately I turn it off and stay stretched out on the couch until much later, when I'm forced to get up and take Lily the Poodle out for a pee, or it's time for a Zoom meeting, or I need to take care of my own pee needs.

I've been on medication for high blood pressure since I was fifty-eight, over twenty-five years now, with no side effects and numbers consistently within a normal range. Maybe my blood pressure's gone out of whack? Back home I don the cuff and check email while it pumps. 121/72, so that's fine. But wait. Heart rate of 42? Isn't that low? I answer a few emails, then check it again. Similar numbers.

My first Dr. Google stop is a "slow heart rate" search at mayoclinic.org. I learn that if the heart beats fewer than 60 times a minute, it has an official disease label: Bradycardia. It can be a serious problem if the heart doesn't pump enough oxygen-rich blood to the body. It's important to get a prompt, accurate diagnosis and appropriate care. Should I worry?

The list of symptoms includes fainting, dizziness, fatigue, shortness of breath, chest pains, confusion or memory problems, and tiring easily during physical activity. So I have two of the symptoms: fatigue and tiring easily while I was walking. But isn't that just one symptom? Maybe I should count confusion or memory problems also, since my short-term memory is shot, but that's been going on for a lot longer than this past month or so. At least I *think* it's been going on for a lot longer. I can't remember for sure.

I continue to monitor my heart rate throughout the weekend. Monday morning, Memorial Day, I send a non-urgent email to my primary care physician telling her my heart rate has been in the low 40s for several days, and that I have no symptoms other than fatigue.

Tuesday morning I get a call from Dr. Kline's office saying she wants to see me. Can I come in at 2:00? I say yes, but think, "Shit." Why should I, in the midst of a pandemic, go to a large medical complex full of sick people? But I get myself together, grab a mask, my iPad for reading in the waiting room, and head out the door.

The usually busy parking structure is nearly empty. I secure my mask and take the reassuringly empty elevator to the second floor. At the door to Internal Medicine I'm met by two attendants in scrubs. While one takes my temperature with a touchless forehead thermometer, the other asks Covid-19 screening questions—have I had contact (defined as being within six feet for more than 15 minutes) or various other forms of personal contact with anyone who has been diagnosed with Covid-19? Do I have fever or chills, cough, shortness of breath, muscle or body aches, a recent onset of loss of taste or smell, etc.? When I've answered all questions to their satisfaction, the attendant uses a pair of tweezers to pull a mask from the pile sitting on the table. She dangles it toward me.

"We want you to use our masks," she explains.

Entering the waiting room, I'm immediately motioned to the counter to check in, and to answer the same Covid-19 screening questions I just answered in the hallway. Moments later I'm called to follow a nurse down the long corridor. It's the usual—state my birthdate, stand on the scale, take a seat to have my vitals taken. This time, though, before those things can happen, I must answer the same damned questions all over again.

Finally, the oxygen measuring device is on my index finger. The blood pressure cuff tightens around my arm. The nurse records the numbers, then says she'd like to take my blood pressure again. She then takes my pulse the old fashioned way. The mood shifts from humdrum routine to intense watchfulness.

"Any shortness of breath?" she asks. "Dizziness? Fainting spells?" and on down the list. No. No. No. Only fatigue, I tell her.

She gestures toward the room in which the doctor will see me, and watches closely as I stand.

"May I take your arm?" she asks.

I shrug. "Sure."

I barely have time to change into the standard gown when the nurse is back with a technician, who wheels a machine into the room. The nurse explains that Dr. Kline wants an EKG. A series of electrodes are stuck to my chest, arms, side, seemingly everywhere. Once wires are attached to the electrodes, the EKG machine steadily spits data out onto orange graph paper.

Dr. Kline comes in as the EKG clicks to a stop. She greets me, takes the graph, gives it a quick glance, thanks the attendant and nurse, who then leave. I try to read her face as she turns her attention back to the EKG. Is that slight frown an indication of trouble, or just part of her usual demeanor? The doctor I thought would see me to the end, the one whose face I could read, suddenly changed jobs about a year ago, and I've only seen Dr. Kline twice before today.

She pulls the email up on the ever-present computer, asks some clarifying questions, then tells me the range of things that may be causing the slow heart rate. It could be an electrical problem. The heart beat is controlled by the sinoatrial node, which may no longer be functioning properly. That condition can be treated with a pacemaker. Also, though, there's a spot on the EKG that may (or may not) indicate some sort of blockage.

"So let's get you to the hospital and work on getting you better."

Wait!! Hospital???

"Really?" I say. "The hospital?"

"Yes," she says, then goes over it all again. The need for thorough diagnostics, prompt treatment . . .

"The hospital?? In the midst of a pandemic?"

"Coronavirus cases are isolated. Stringent protocols are in place," she assures me.

I tell her I'm not great with medical details and would like to call my retired nurse sister-in-law for a three-way conversation. Dr. Kline agrees. I call Marg and put her on speaker phone. I again hear the same information, hear Marg's questions and responses, and am persuaded. I thank Marg for her help, ask that she let my kids know what's up, and end the call.

Dr. Kline assures me that this is absolutely the right thing to do and says she'll call for transport.

"My car's just downstairs," I tell her.

"You drove here by yourself??"

I repeat that I feel fine, just tired. *She* repeats that people with such low heart rates often suffer from dizzy spells or, worse yet, lose consciousness. And so it is that I soon find myself strapped to a gurney in a semi-seated position, being rolled down the hall, into the elevator, and out into a waiting ambulance. This would be a great opportunity to give the queen's wave, except the halls are virus-empty, as is the parking lot.

At the hospital, after more Covid questions, a new mask, and signing something I don't read, I'm admitted. I'm pretty sure what I signed says I'll be forever financially responsible for whatever huge sums of money my insurance doesn't kick in with, and if they kill or maim me neither I nor my next of kin can sue them. Oh well.

In a curtained cubby, a friendly nurse, Kathy, asks the same old, now *truly* boring, questions, helps me into a hospital gown, adjusts the bed, puts my clothes and purse in a large plastic bag with handles, and hooks me up to a blood pressure monitor that automatically squeezes my arm every ten minutes. Kathy leaves to fetch a glass of water for me and a technician wheels in another EKG machine. Kathy returns with a lidded cup of water complete with hospital straw, rearranges and adds to the existing EKG stickers, connects the wires, and the machine kicks out yet another graph measuring what my heart is—or is not—up to.

Next, a team of cardiologists, all wearing masks and green scrubs, fill the cubby. There's the Top Doc, older and with an impressive title, and three others, younger, who are residents. TD sits in a chair, facing me, while the three students listen attentively from the other side of my bed. TD is relaxed, friendly, as he asks a string of questions that have become almost as repetitive as the Covid questions. Any shortness of breath? Chest pain? Dizziness? Arrhythmia? Lost consciousness? Feeling faint? Have I fallen recently? No, no, no, no. Only tired.

"It's a good sign that you're conscious and talking to me, and that you're coherent," he says, smiling. At least his eyes indicate he might be smiling. His lips are hidden behind his mask.

He listens to my heart, checks my pulse, studies the EKG for a moment, then confirms what Dr. Kline said earlier. Low heart rate—bradycardia. It may simply be a problem with the sinoatrial node, the heart's natural pacemaker, in which case the surgical insertion of a mechanical pacemaker just under the skin can regulate my heartbeat.

On the other hand, a blockage or damaged heart tissue will require more extensive treatment. A cardiac catheterization, also known as an angiogram, will give a picture of what's going on and may include an intervention in the form of one or more stents. But a pacemaker may do the trick. It often does.

Since it's now nearly 6:00, the procedure won't happen until tomorrow. TD tells me that Dr. Lee, who he indicates with a nod, will go over this process in greater detail. He and the other two doctors leave the room.

Dr. Lee is young and trim. What I can see of his face is unlined. He first describes in detail the pacemaker process. He speaks slowly and clearly, using both technical and lay terms. By this time, though, I'm hungry, tired, and my brain may be following my heart's lead on the path to sluggishness. Whether he's talking about veins or arteries, or the right or left chambers of the heart, doesn't

mean much to me. What I *do* comprehend is that
during the procedure a tube will be inserted in an
artery or vein in either my wrist or groin
(YIKES!) and guided along from a small electronic device to my heart. The electronic device,
the pacemaker, will be placed under the skin just
below my collarbone, probably on the left side.
I'll be given something to reduce pain and aid in
relaxation, but general anesthesia is not required.

The procedure is extremely low risk, though
any intrusive procedure risks possible heart at-
tack, stroke, bleeding, etc. However, in a study of
over 50,000 patients, the rate of death directly re-
lated to the pacemaker procedures was 0.10%. I'm
briefly distracted trying to figure out whether
that means a mortality rate of 10 out of 100,000,
or 100 out of 100,000.

Do I have any questions? I shake my head no,
knowing that my questions are of an existential
nature and beyond young Dr. Lee's field of expertise. He says he'll see me in the morning before
surgery, and slips through the curtain. Nurse
Kathy returns, checks monitors, says she's ordered dinner to be delivered to my room, puts my
bag of belongings on the foot of the bed, and
checks to be sure I'm in a comfortable position.
She is charming and considerate, laughs at my
jokes, and I think maybe I should follow the
standard advice for oldsters to cultivate younger
friends. Maybe I should invite her to our

neighborhood's next, safely-spaced, "Dinner on the Green."

John, in burgundy scrubs, arrives to wheel me upstairs to the Cardiac Intensive Care unit. Kathy walks along beside . . . Wait. Cardiac Intensive Care? It's beginning to sink in that my condition is risky.

In CICU, Kathy introduces me to Betty, my new nurse, sings my praises as the number one best patient, sings Betty's praises to me, and leaves. I'm disappointed that my friendship with Kathy is so quickly nipped in the bud, especially since Betty seems a bit dour. I remind myself that her major job is not to charm me, but to take care of business, which she is doing.

On a small white board on the wall opposite the foot of my bed, Betty writes "Nurse: Betty." Below that, after "Contact," she fills in my brother's name and phone numbers. Explaining everything as she goes, she replaces the sticky electrode patches, sets up the blood pressure cuff, checks the IV connection, and completes other mysterious medical tech things.

Having had a light breakfast and only an apple and cheese for lunch, my stomach is growling its complaints. I tell Betty that Kathy ordered dinner for me and I'm more than ready for a bite to eat. She goes to check on food and I take the opportunity to call Dale.

"Hey, Marilyn!"

I catch him up on the basics.

"What a revoltin' development this is!" he says, quoting an old radio show character.

I tell him I'll be having surgery for a pacemaker tomorrow. "Zero point one percent fatality rate."

"Better odds than I've got driving to Folsom today," he laughs. He asks how I'm feeling, tells me he's got a text thread going with family and friends, and that he'll catch everyone up. The hospital records include a signed POLST (Physician Orders for Life-Sustaining Treatment). Even so, I confirm with Dale, who has medical power of attorney for me, that if things go wrong, I want no artificial means of nutrition including feeding tubes, no CPR, only treatment for the sake of comfort.

"Got it," he says. "Need anything?"

"Drop by with a martini?"

Betty returns, minus a dinner tray.

"I'll catch up with you tomorrow morning, after I've talked with the doctor," I tell him, then turn my attention to Betty.

She tells me there's no dinner waiting for me and the kitchen is now closed, but she'll see what she can find. She's soon back with a ham and cheese sandwich, and small cartons of orange juice and milk, neither of which I like.

"I'm sorry," she says. "This is the best I could do."

I thank her, impressed that she's gone out of her way to find something for me. I'm beginning to realize that if one must be in a hospital, the CICU is the place to be. One patient to a room. One nurse to a patient. The luxury of this care is not lost on me, nor the luxury of knowing it's covered by insurance. The sandwich though—whatever image comes to mind when you read "ham and cheese sandwich," forget it. What's on my plate consists of something the color and texture of light cardboard, plus a slice of ham thin enough that I could lay it out on my iPad screen and read a book through it! I'm hungry though, so I give it a try. Two stick-to-the-roof-of-my-mouth bites, softened by two sips of milk, and I'm done. It's not like it's going to kill me to miss a meal.

When Betty sees how little I've eaten she suggests I might want to take a few more bites.

"After midnight tonight, there's no food until after your procedure."

I pick up the "sandwich," then set it back down.

"It's okay. I'm hoping for a little weight loss as a fringe benefit."

When I tell her that I'm cold, Betty brings socks and a heated blanket. My disappointment with losing Nurse Kathy wanes as I experience Betty's professional competence and accessibility.

When I was first admitted, having read descriptions of cotton swabs forced through nostrils into the cranial cavity, I declined the recommended Covid-19 test. But in order to have any invasive procedure, I must first be tested for the dreaded virus. Betty does the deed. As much as she tries to be gentle, it is a reminder that nearly anything can be used as an instrument of torture, including cotton swabs.

For the sake of possible sleep, Betty adjusts the automatic blood pressure monitor to record every hour rather than every ten minutes. After untangling my blankets, straightening my loose hospital gown, and handing me the remote that will allow me to adjust the bed's tilt to my liking, she tells me the doctor ordered a potassium drip—it may sting a little. "A little" doesn't begin to describe it. I give it a few minutes, hoping the sting will ease. It doesn't. I press the call button and Betty is with me within moments.

"This is really painful," I tell her.

She says that slowing the drip sometimes helps. She makes an adjustment, tells me to call if I need to, and leaves. I hope for some relief but it doesn't come. My arm is on fire from wrist to elbow. I practice deep breathing. I focus on gently rolling ocean waves and pine trees in mountains. I vow to give it at least five minutes before I call again. But why? Between deep breaths, nature scenes, and clock-watching, I review my typical responses to pain.

I was raised to downplay aches and pains. "Practice a little Christian Science," my mother would tell me. My Aunt Alice, my mother's sister-in-law, was a devout Christian Scientist and although her views on the nonexistence of physical infirmity were held in contempt by the rest of the family, my mother somehow thought that they should apply to me. I don't think I ever actually heard the words "get over it," but the attitude was deeply ingrained. As a result, or maybe coincidentally, my sensitivity to pain is at the lower end of the scale. I go to a massage therapist whenever I can barely turn my head an inch to the left. She asks me: when did this start? I don't know. What's your pillow like? Ummm. Medium? Does heat help? Don't know. Ice? Don't know.

So here's what I *do* know. I'm not overreacting to the fire in my arm. I ring for Betty.

"I can't tolerate this," I say.

Thankfully, she doesn't tell me to use a little Christian Science. She removes the drip. Next there's a magnesium drip. Not so bad. Once that's completed, I can move to a more comfortable position.

I doze off and on. During periods of wakefulness I wonder what's in store for me tomorrow. Might I be one of the 0.10% that checks out as doctors are messing about in my chest cavity? Nearly eighty-five, I've already beaten the longevity odds. Although there are some things that I would do differently given a second chance, I am generally at peace with how I've lived my life. My "Final Exit" file is in order and the major players know where to find it. I've not yet completed the list of songs I want played at my going away party, but all of the important documents and information are there. And even if death is just around the corner for me, I will still have had more than my share of life.

Insomnia—The Dirty Dozen

It's strange how some dates stay in my mind long after they're needed. My mother's birthday, my father's birthday, their anniversary, the birthday of my now long dead best friend from junior high school. Today is the 65th anniversary of my marriage to my first husband. I remember that, but have to check the birthday list every April for the exact date of my granddaughter's birthday. And is she twenty-five or twenty-six? It would be much better to remember that than the date of that 65th wedding anniversary, better to remember her sister's birthdate than my father's, better to remember her parents' wedding anniversary than the wedding anniversary of my own parents.

Last night, during my habitual three a.m. sleeplessness, "The Dirty Dozen" intruded on my musings. Not that old "Dirty Dozen" war movie, but my parents' pinochle group that, for decades, got together monthly to play cards and eat dessert. The group consisted of cousins and their spouses. Not that it can possibly matter to anyone reading this, but the cousins are the first named in each couple: Esther and Fay, my parents; Thomas and Alice, my mother's brother and his wife; Faye and Melvin; Russell and Hazel; Ethel and George; and . . . and . . . shit! Who was that other couple??

My logical brain tells me it makes absolutely no difference in the overall scheme of things whether I can remember their names or not. Relax. Go back to sleep. But underneath the logic, something is churning away, bringing a sense of desperation to the missing names.

During this particular morning's three a.m. time slot, I'm seeing the group from the vantage point of a four, maybe five-year-old. I'm leaning against the archway between the living room and dining room. I have to crane my neck to see faces. My straight-ahead view is only of knees. I can hear the high-pitched giggly voice of Cousin (oh, what was her name?) and picture her. Plump—now there's a word you don't hear much anymore—in a flowered jersey dress and chunky heels. And her husband, bland in his beige suit, with his beige hair and light beige face. My mother is wearing a dark blue velvet dress. Contrary to what might come to mind from the Dirty Dozen label, they got dressed up for these pinochle games, the men all in suits and ties, the women in their Sunday best.

Uncle George sidles up next to my mother and rubs her sleeve between thumb and forefinger. "I sure like the feel of velvet," he tells her, in what I now know was a suggestive tone. Back then I thought it was funny because my mother laughed. Funny, too, that my Aunt Ethel, Uncle George's wife, did a shaming finger move, sing-song saying "Now, Georgie Porgie . . ." If Uncle

George were still alive, would he garner attention from women in the "Me Too" movement?

But what *was* the name of that other couple? If I can get the name of one, I'll get the name of the other. I suddenly remember that the plump, giggly cousin was the one my father hated to be partnered with. She didn't pay attention to the cards, forgot what suit they'd bid in, threw away trump cards willy-nilly. But what the fuck was her name?

None of the Dirty Dozen ever said "fuck." I'd bet next month's retirement check on it. All of the cousins were churchgoers who regularly attended a Disciples of Christ Church in Alhambra, the church they all grew up in. All but my parents. They'd moved to Temple City, out beyond civilization, and the only church in town other than the Catholic Church, was a Methodist church. That's where they sent me on Sundays.

Elinor!!! Elinor and Ray!! Whew! What a relief. I fluff my pillow and turn on my side, certain that with the emergence of the mystery couples' names, sleep will come.

Half a Dog is Better Than None

A sunny Saturday morning in October, 2021. The white mostly-miniature-poodle bounds into the house, followed closely by Roger, my dog-sharing partner. Lily's been with him for the past five days and now it's my turn.

She pauses long enough for me to give her a quick head scratch, then rushes to the laundry room to check her food bowl. Nothing there. A quick sip of water, a circling of the living room, sniffing corners, toenails click, click, clicking on the hardwood floors.

"Time for a cup of tea?" I ask.

Roger checks his watch. "Better not," he says. "I still haven't finished writing tomorrow's sermon. She peed and pooped about an hour ago, breakfast around 7:15," he says, then, "Bye, Lily! Bye, Baby!" his voice pitched an octave higher than usual. He gives her a quick ruffle and is out the door. She follows.

"Lily, Lily, you're with me," I call after her. She turns, runs back inside.

I bring her bed from the top of the dryer to the rug in front of the kitchen slider—her favorite place. I give her a Greenie, one of the very few treats she likes. She takes it to her bed and settles in. I put a pee pad on the floor in front of the washer. On the rare times she pees inside, that's the place she chooses, so best to be safe.

We adopted her together from Foothill Dog Rescue, a little over five years ago. After a brief period of adjustment, Lily easily adapted to our shared dog-custody routines. She generally gets more treats when she's with me than when she's with Roger, and maybe more doting. But she has more people interactions and free-range time when she's with him at church, plus his house is busier than mine. Whatever the differences, she seems happy with either one of us.

I take Lily's travel bag to the laundry/dog supply room and unpack it. There is a partially used can of Newman's Own Dinner for Dogs, chicken and rice recipe, in a thermal bag. A large plastic baggie contains grooming supplies; a seldom-to-never used, lethal-looking, steel-toothed undercoat de-matter; a rubber pet shampoo brush (another seldom used tool); a more regularly used bristle brush; a toothbrush with which to clean Lily's poodle tears; and a fine-tooth comb to separate the wispy hairs that get matted together around her teary eyes. Another baggie holds her twice daily anti-seizure meds.

On a typical Lily day, she'll ride with me in the car while I run errands, or sleep by my desk as I check email, work on some writing project, take a turn on my online Scrabble game, or indulge in long searches with Ms. Google. I probably spend more time at the computer than is healthy, but Lily at least gets me out of my chair every couple of hours when she needs to go outside.

In the afternoons, I often stretch out on the chaise in my office to read, and maybe nap. Lily naps beside me. Our lives could be labeled dull and uneventful, but Lily seems quite happy with dull and uneventful, as am I.

~

When Sunny, a miniature schnauzer, died back in 2013, I missed her terribly. She'd been Mike's idea. Every other dog I'd had growing up and all through adulthood had been a rescue dog. I was resistant to the idea of paying a four-figure price for a purebred pup but it was Mike's turn to choose, and I agreed to go with him to the breeders to see the most recent litter. (No doubt you've already guessed the end of *this* story.)

Although I loved Sunny and often took her on walks, she was mostly Mike's dog. He was the one who fed her, took her to the vet and to the groomer, the one she most successfully begged food from. Then, sometime in 2009, Mike's Frontotemporal Dementia had advanced to the stage where he couldn't remember if he'd fed her. She was quick to take advantage, to stand in front of him, barking, until he fed her again. And again. I took to hiding the dog food after the first morning feeding, which was—as were so many details of everyday life—extremely frustrating to Mike. The time came in late 2010 when I could no longer safely manage him, and out of necessity, moved him to a residential memory care facility. Then Sunny became fully my dog.

This was the saddest, most difficult time of my life, and Sunny was my constant, ever-attentive, ever-cheerful companion.

For months after she died, I'd get glimpses of her as I walked past her favorite sunny spot in front of the coffee table. I continued to "hear" the sound of her quick, early morning wake-up bark long after she was gone. Slowly though, her absence became a reality and I, never without a dog in all of my then seventy-nine years, struggled with being dog-less.

There was the expense of a dog—food, vet bills, grooming, supplies, pet sitting for the occasional trip out of town. Also, given my age, there was the distinct possibility that whatever dog I might get would outlive me. Or, I could get an old dog, but that, too, would have its problems. So, no dog.

Damn it, though! I had to sleep alone. Walk alone. I had no one with whom to watch TV. Worse yet, no one to play with! I didn't like being without a dog. I reviewed my list of reasons not to get a dog. It mostly boiled down to money. My monthly teacher's retirement check covers basic necessities with enough left for an occasional dinner out or a rare weekend trip, but there's not much wiggle room. But . . . wait a minute! What if

I shared a dog??? I was pretty sure I could afford half a dog. It would have to be the right person though. Should I advertise on Nextdoor? The geography would work … but on second thought, I'd read too many nutcase posts to feel confident I'd find a mentally balanced dog-sharing partner.

I considered the necessary requirements for my dog sharer. It would need to be someone with an easygoing personality, no alarmists. He or she should live within ten miles of me, preferably closer. It would have to be a trustworthy person who would pay their share and take good care of the dog when it was his/her turn as dog guardian.

And it would have to be someone whose preferred dog qualities were similar to mine. I'd want a small to medium-sized dog. Not one of those tiny freaks of nature that you can hold in the palm of your hand. *Normal* small, say around 15 pounds, to medium size, maybe around 25. I'll say that: 15-25 pounds. House-trained. Preferably female. Preferably non-shedder, though neither male nor shedder would be a deal breaker if I fell in love. I'd want to find a vet who practices as if it were 1950. No back surgery or chemotherapy that runs into thousands and thousands of dollars. No heroic measures. Both my dog partner and I should do obedience training so we'd be using a similar approach.

Once the dog sharing possibility occurred to me, I started looking at every friend I met for coffee, every neighbor on the street, every co-writer in my writing workshops, as a potential dog sharer. As has so often been the case in my life, the universe, or Mimi Avocada or fate, or whatever, gave me a boost. I had dropped by the church office to deliver something, and while chatting with Roger, I mentioned my desire to share a dog.

"My friends keep telling me I should get a dog so I'd have someone to cuddle with at night," he said.

Hmmm. Roger lives and works nearby. He's a responsible person, likely in sync with my "no heroic measures" stance. Old enough to be settled and mature, young enough that the dog will still have a home after my demise.

We talked. We agreed that we'd like a non-shedding, female, house-trained, medium-sized dog, though we'd be open to variations. No frou-frou dogs. We both thought we should be getting in more daily steps; a dog would encourage longer walks. Maybe an older dog more in need of a home? Because of my experiences with Sunny, my preference was for a schnauzer, or part schnauzer.

Here's the kind of email we had flying back and forth.

Me, 5/31/15: Under the right circumstances, it would be ideal to share a dog, sort of like a shared child custody arrangement ... I'm thinking we would each have the dog for one or two weeks at a time, and cover for each other when one or the other of us needs to be away ... I have a soft spot for Miniature Schnauzers—medium sized non-shedders ... Your thoughts??

P.S. This may be a cockamamie idea. I won't be offended if you're not interested, but I think you and I would likely be compatible co-custodians.

Roger: I think shared custody is a very good idea especially if we don't have to get divorced first to get to that stage. I haven't had a dog since I was a kid and I do enjoy them. I was concerned about my hardwood floors (newly redone) and my absences and long days and also the cost, especially of medical care. Sharing a dog with you would help on costs and avoid the hassle and cost of boarding dogs. I feel there is something wrong with a society in which lots of people pay tens of thousands for medical care for pets but we let people suffer without enough access, and also with the low affordability of housing juxtaposed with 40 dollar doggie hotels. These concerns help me rationalize putting off getting a dog, but if I had one, I'd rationalize it in some other way. Perhaps that it would keep me sane ... some of the rescue schnauzers are cute. Though ... there is something about their facial hair that reminds me of some eccentric men I haven't liked. However, I can imagine if I met prospective adoptees and one with the right personality and recommendation letters made a pitch for my affection, I could get to love it. Are there any other breeds that fit the smaller, shed-free, vigilant but social criteria for you?

I shared with Roger my history with dogs, all rescue mutts with the exception of Sunny, and all wonderful dogs—there was Brownie, the shepherd mix who was already on the scene before I was born. Although I obviously don't remember this, my mother told me that when I was a baby, whenever I cried in my room, Brownie would race in and pace back and forth under my crib. He was just the right height to jiggle the mattress and quiet me.

When I was nine and Brownie was twelve, he was called to doggie heaven and Stocky came to live with me. Stocky, short for "Stockade." A small, smooth-haired terrier mix, she'd been born in an army stockade where Bob, my aunt's soldier boyfriend, was spending a few days for an offense that was not spoken of within the range of my young ears. Bob saved Stocky from death by drowning by bringing her to my grandmother.

She happily rode in my bicycle basket when I went everywhere but to school, slept on my bed and, like Brownie had been, was a good listener. She died when I was twenty, shortly before my first marriage.

Earlier on, I told you that I'd never in my whole life been without a dog but if you're a stickler for accuracy, I'll admit that I *was* dogless once, but only for a few months. Pete and I married in March of 1956 and moved into a small one-bedroom upstairs apartment in the town where we'd both grown up. We each had fulltime jobs and we weren't thinking of a dog, but a week before my September birthday, Pete came home with a black, mostly cocker spaniel pup, another soon-to-be drowned rescue. "Happy Birthday," Pete said, as he brought the pup into the kitchen and handed her to me. We named her Shadow and, though we hadn't *planned* on a dog, we fell in love with her and adapted our lives to meet her needs. She was the dog our daughters grew up with. Shadow lasted much longer in my life than Pete did, but that's another story.

After Shadow, there was Zoltan. Then Thorn. Then Sadie, And finally, Sunny. Roger's dog history was much shorter.

> *Roger, 6/6/15: I like mutts as well, especially those that have some features of cute breeds. We had a mixed dog with some toy collie in her, my older brother's dog, and she was the best dog, except for the shedding. We also had a beagle that was the runt of the litter and afraid of everyone. Mom was the alpha and he feared the males of the house, in sequence, with me as the least dangerous. I still think*

they are cute as heck but they howl and I don't need any pure breed. I agree with NO poodles (or at least not with traditional grooming) and NO slobbery ones. Today at the Pride Festival, the Front Street Shelter had a booth with a dog being fostered, a 1.5 year old terrier mix that was the sweetest thing. They were pushing "adopt one now for $25 instead of $85 and we throw in a first vet visit free." Fortunately, many others came up and fell all over themselves so I could make a clean break and come back to my senses.

For much of July, Roger was out of town; I was in and out during August, so the dog search was temporarily on hold. With September came the browsing of various sites followed by in-person visits. The local animal shelters were filled with pitbulls and Chihuahaus, both of which were a far cry from our wish list. The few medium-sized dogs that came through the shelters were scooped up in the blink of an eye. It was frustrating. By February we were still looking.

Me, 2/11/16: My feeling is that we might find a better match if we looked at rescue sites where dogs are being fostered and where we'd learn more about temperament, whether or not they're housebroken, possible behavioral problems, etc. One of our reasons for searching shelters is that those dogs really need a home. But since the non-pitbull/Chihuahuas go so quickly, we needn't feel guilty if we find a dog somewhere else.

Roger: This makes sense and is fortuitous because I have got a Doberman for us. And because they had a 2-for-1 special, I also got a sled dog, a veteran of a (losing) Iditarod race. At a friend's recommendation, we decided to visit the Foothill Dog Rescue group in Shingle Springs.

Me: Should we take the Doberman and sled dog with us and surrender them to the rescuers?

Roger: We can attach the sled dog to the Prius. And use the Doberman to make them give us the puppy we want!

The dog rescue site was about thirty miles away in a strip mall. It consisted of two large rooms, one for small dogs and one for large dogs, wandering about or in separate pens with several dog fostering attendants. The site was crowded with potential, pre-approved dog owners. When we first wandered into the room, a rambunctious black terrier took to Roger, bouncing around him, pausing to be petted, and looking lovingly into his eyes. Roger fell in Love. I fell in Like. Male. A shedder. He didn't quite fit our criteria but his personality made up for it. Sadly though, when we asked to take him outside to get better acquainted, we found he'd been adopted moments before.

An attendant suggested we meet Lily, a white, mostly miniature poodle mix. We followed them outside. Lily stayed close behind the attendant while we got her statistics. Six weeks ago, she'd been rescued from a kill shelter in Modesto and had been in foster care since then. The foster "parent" thought Lily was now ready for adoption. She'd been with their family on a large piece of property. She was house-trained, shy, and liked children. We walked with her a short way, petted her, talked to her. She *was* shy but, according to the attendant, she would soon warm up. She seemed sweet. Except that she was mostly poodle, she met our wish list—right size, non-shedding, female, house-trained. We agreed that we could de-froufrou her by avoiding poodle cuts.

The vet's report said that she'd had seizures but they were controlled by medication. The cost of the medication was around $15.00 a month, so: doable. We closed the deal and made arrangements to pick her up the next day, February 13. Then the details of dog sharing started in earnest—establishing a connection with a local vet, deciding who does what with her when, sharing information.

Me, 2/27/21: You asked about recent expenses. The tear cleansing solution was

$15.00 and the probiotic spray was $15.00 plus $4.00 shipping, so a total of $34.00, or $17.00 each. As for grooming, let's plan to take turns getting her groomed every 6-8 weeks. How are we doing the trade off this time? I can pick her up sometime Sunday or Monday, whatever is convenient. I'll be leaving very early Thursday morning and returning Saturday evening so she's yours again Wednesday night. If you can manage it, it would be good for you to join us for dog training at 5:00 Wednesday evening, so we can be consistent. Thanks for sharing—Marilyn

Roger, 2/27/21: Hi, Marilyn, and thanks for the yogurt and for the info here. It's amusing to see her stretch and get her land legs when she first gets up . . . I was going to miss the training due to three meetings in a row on Wednesday, but I realize that she won't have much reinforcement if I miss it. Is the training over at 6:00? Would you prefer to have her Sunday afternoon or Monday late morning? I know Monday gives you only two nights together, so let me know your preference! She was a big hit with church staff and also with my colleague when we met for coffee downtown. Yours, R.

When we got her, Lily was afraid of other dogs and somewhat wary of people. According to her papers, she had been picked up off the streets as a stray. The picture taken at the Modesto facility shows a very thin, bedraggled, scared-looking dog. At first, she would cringe when I reached down to pat her head. She always brightened at the sight of a child, though, and might have benefitted from a placement that included children. Unfortunately, I was far beyond child-bearing age and Roger, as a 50- to 60-ish single gay man, was an unlikely candidate for parenthood, so Lily was sentenced to our two childless homes. She did receive the added perk of hanging out with Roger at work in his church office where a variety of people were constantly in and out, all petting and sweet-talking her. She gradually warmed up and became less skittish.

When Lily was with me, we went for short walks in the neighborhood and sometimes met up with a child or two. Because she's small with soft, fluffy hair, and isn't a jumper, she appeals to little kids. From the beginning, though, she didn't like walks on the leash and strained to go back home.

Roger and I settled into regular Lily-related communications.

Me: 2/11/16: I hope your Colorado time has been good—productive, renewing, whatever you hoped for . . . This coming Saturday morning I'll be flying to Palm Springs to celebrate my cousin's remarriage to her first husband. I'll be away from early Saturday morning to

Monday night. Are you okay to have Lily during that time?

Tonight is an obedience training session. Gulp! The assignment was to sit, treat, repeat; stand, treat, repeat; down, treat, repeat; walk one step, stop, have dog sit, treat, repeat, etc. with stand and down. Have stay, stand and down last for one full minute by tonight's class. Lily and I are only good with sit. I hope we won't be wearing dunce caps by the end of the session.

Me: 3/29/16: Lily and I are scheduled for the third Good Manners class tomorrow evening. It starts at 5:00 in the Sacramento Animal Hospital parking lot. If you're free, please join us.

Roger, 3/29/16: Hi, M and L. I should go so she can't pull a fast one on me anymore, but getting there by 5 is tough. I'll see! . . . Maybe I'll take her to the groomer next to the Foothill Rescue place next Wed or Thurs AM or Friday the 8th. I have a haircut that afternoon myself!

And so it went. When it first occurred to me that dog sharing might be a possibility, I was envisioning a regular schedule, say Saturday to Saturday. It turned out that neither Roger nor I had predictable enough schedules for such a plan. If one of us had been rigid about time shifts and the other not, that would have been trouble. Luckily, both of us were comfortable with a more spontaneous approach.

And it soon became clear that Lily was not going to encourage us to take long walks. She was actually *almostly* house-trained. Playing was of no interest to her. Roll a ball near her and she gave no response. Put a soft animal toy in her bed and she seemed not to notice. But she was sweet and cute, and adapted easily to our shared custody routines. As for pickup and delivery, I live within two miles of the church and within three miles of Roger's home. Sundays were often easy exchange days. I could bring Lily to church, leave her in Roger's office and she'd go home with him, or vice-versa. Or, Roger would swing by my place on his way to work. We were well matched geographically. And Lily loved car rides.

There were always details to manage. Sometimes Roger and I figured things out through phone calls, or texts, or in person during exchange times. Much of the time, though, we clarified schedules and other plans through emails.

Me, 3/24/18: I had a dog door put into the door that leads outside from my laundry room. $16.00. With practice and lots of treats, Lily learned to use it the day after it was installed. I smeared the anti-flea/tick potion on her this afternoon. We're working on "stay. She's good for several seconds so that's a start. Also I'm sending a baggie of her old food for you to *mix with the new stuff. I think about 1/2 and 1/2 for a week should do it. I'll get a bag of Taste of the Wild before my next stint with her. Mid-day tomorrow is fine.*

Roger, 3/25/18: Glad you found a solution for the doorway. Thanks for anointing Lily. Are you coming this way? If not, I can come and get her at noon . . .

An added fringe benefit of having Lily in my life is that Roger is also more in my life than he would otherwise have been. The whole dog-sharing process is something of a bonding experience.

But back to this sunny October Saturday: A little after 5:00, I pour a glass of Chardonnay, put a few slices of jack cheese on a small plate along with an equally few crackers. Lily watches, dancing around me on her hind legs.

"Happy Hour," I tell her, and the dance moves from a fast waltz to hip hop. I maneuver my way around the dancing dog to take my treats out to the patio table, then go back to retrieve Lily's. She didn't like the beef jerky treats I got for her last week until I slathered them in peanut butter and froze them. Now, they're a hit.

It's in the mid-eighties, my favorite outdoor temperature. The recent fires are under control, leaving the Sacramento air smoke-free. I sip wine and nibble cheese while reading the evening news on my iPad. Lily lies at my feet, happily munching her peanut butter-laden beef jerky. A humming-bird flits around the feeder that hangs from the apple tree. It is a lovely evening. I'm saddened by the world around us. Covid deaths, homelessness, the overwhelming number of people displaced by wars and famines, the rage that exists in our divided nation, but ah, it's Happy Hour here on my patio with Lily. All is well. Later in the evening, she dozes next to me on the couch as I watch the latest episode of "Ted Lasso," followed by "The Kominsky Method."

At bedtime, I pull the pet steps up to the side of the bed. Lily waits politely to be invited up. I grab a tiny trainer treat, settle into bed, and tap the top step. Lily climbs up. I give her the treat and she takes her place beside me. Stretched out with *Homeland Elegies* on my iPad, I feel the slightest bit of Lily pressure against my lower leg. That's where she'll be until somewhere near seven when I'll hear her first tentative move onto the pet steps and rush to lead her out for her morning pee.

In many ways, Lily falls short of our early ideal dog list. But we were right all of those years ago when Roger and I allowed as how we'd fall in love with whatever dog we ended up with. And it turns out that falling in love in one's eighties is a great gift, even if the object of one's love is only half a dog.

~

Afterthoughts: Although this is *my* book and I get to decide what goes into it, Roger has persuaded me that, as an equal sharer, he has the right to express a different perspective:

I have had second thoughts about my appearance in your memoir. I believe that our shared canine should be, for her dignity's sake and mine, described as an Irish setter of impeccable discipline, who barks only at intruders or the smoke alarm, who sits at the door to go out to pee, who eats all food presented, who frolics with neighbor dogs and who wears us out with her indefatigable walking of the neighborhood, where neighbors greet us with warm words of praise that mask their envy of our good fortune, dedication and skill. So, stop the presses . . .

Random Thoughts at 3:00 a.m.

Early this morning, aphorisms floated to consciousness. I don't know why. A few weeks ago, it was memories of the Dirty Dozen. And some time recently, my mind was trying to come up with exceptions to the rule "When two vowels go walking, the first one does the talking." Well . . . earth, bear, about, shout, out, good, food, friend, poise, and on and on. Such things have absolutely no importance in my life, yet once they come to mind, they demand attention. Is this a function of old age? I don't think my early morning musings were always so random. Maybe these thoughts take up the space where I used to worry about my kids as they were growing up. I don't worry about them now; they've got good work, they take good care of the grandkids.

And Mike, finally released from the prison of Frontotemporal Dementia. I no longer need to worry about his condition, his state of being or non-being, or how to pay for the secure memory care facility. And students. I no longer need to worry about troubled—or troubling—students. So maybe it's that there's free 3:00 a.m. space that needs to be filled? Whatever the reason, it was aphorisms this morning.

It may have started when I remembered my determination to get up early. "Early to bed, early to rise, makes a man healthy, wealthy, and wise." Sexist, but to say "makes a woman healthy..." messes with the rhythm. "Makes them healthy, wealthy, and wise" is a better fit and currently more politically correct. But then, it was a quick jump to "The early bird gets the worm." Then: "A bird in the hand is worth two in the bush," and on to: "Kill two birds with one stone." And then, "Birds of a feather flock together."

From there on, my thoughts became more agrarian. "The grass is always greener on the other side of the fence," and "You never miss the water til the well runs dry," and "Don't put all your eggs in one basket." Which gets me thinking that most of today's kids probably can't relate to that one, having had no experience with gathering eggs from a hen house. And what about "Stubborn as a mule?" It used to be you could say that about someone and everyone would understand just how stubborn that person was. Have today's young people ever even seen a mule? There are hardly any mules around anymore. There were hundreds of thousands of working mules in this country up until the 1930's when all that farm machinery was invented, and pouf! went the mules. Was it hundreds of thousands? Maybe it was tens of thousands. I should add that to my "Things for Ms. Google" list. Not that it makes any difference, but that's mostly what I like to explore: things that don't make any difference.

How about "You can lead a horse to water, but you can't make it drink?" Who now, in the general public, knows how important it is for a horse to drink when there's opportunity? "High on the hog?" "A hard row to hoe?" "A stitch in time saves nine?" "A watched pot never boils?" How about "You reap what you sow?" Or "A penny saved is a penny earned?" Pennies are nothing these days. No wonder. There's nothing you can buy for a penny anymore. Most people don't even bother to pick them up if they see one on the ground.

How about "Minding your Ps and Qs?" Hardly anyone under the age of sixty even knows what handwritten Ps and Qs look like. A few weeks ago, hands poised over his keyboard, a UPS clerk looked at the address label on the package I wanted to send, looked more closely, then said, "Could you please read this to me? I can't read it." At first, I thought he had some kind of learning disability, but no, he just couldn't read plain simple handwriting. He wouldn't be minding his Ps and Qs. Apparently, my cursive style of handwriting is just one more piece of evidence that I've reached antiquity.

There's "Separating the sheep from the goats," and "Gentle as a lamb." And while we're with the animals, "Don't look a gift horse in the mouth," and "Let sleeping dogs lie," and "You can't teach an old dog new tricks," though a variety of animal studies contradicted *that* idea years ago. There's "The rain falls on everyone, and likewise shines the sun."

So why is it I can remember all of these damned aphorisms but not the name of the new neighbor I met yesterday? Or, worse yet, the title or author of the book I'm currently reading?

And what about the newer expressions? The ones younger people are using? The ones that aren't connected with farm animals, or farm work, or domestic skills.

Maybe "What goes around comes around" will stick. That's not exactly new, though. What else? Doesn't every generation come up with these everyday words of wisdom? I'll be having lunch with twenty-six-year-old Subei next week. Maybe she can enlighten me regarding current aphorisms.

What started me thinking about all of this, anyway? Oh, yeah. Intending to get up early in the morning. But, as we all know, "The road to hell is paved with good intentions."

The Gift of Reading—
Part 1: It Keeps on Giving

"The greatest gift is a passion for reading. It is cheap, it consoles, it distracts, it excites, it gives you knowledge of the world and experience of a wide kind. It is a moral illumination."
~Elizabeth Hardwick

Yesterday morning when I checked email, among the requests for charitable and political donations, various scam attempts, a few messages from friends, Facebook notifications and breaking news, was one of those occasional unexpected gifts from the universe. It was a message on my seldomly-used website from a student who'd been in my English/Reading class close to thirty years ago. Candice hoped that I remembered her, caught me up a bit on her life, reminded me that she'd read an early draft of my teen novel, *Detour for Emmy*, sent good wishes, and included her phone number.

Of course I remembered Candice. At the age of seventeen, after three years at one of the traditional high schools in our district, she'd enrolled at CHS with zero credits in English.

In my English/Reading classes students read something of their choice for twenty to thirty minutes a day, and during the last fifteen minutes of class they wrote a page or so, again on a subject of their choice. And, as happened more often than random chance would predict, Candice quickly connected with a book I'd suggested, *The Bookmaker's Daughter*, by Shirley Abbott. After reflecting on that experience she wrote:

"I had read other interesting books before this one, but this seemed to be a definitive, resounding experience for me unlike any other I had had. And it perhaps more than the book itself, and actually the moment sparkles to me still because I believe that the book triggered in me my then nascent love of language and the resplendent permanence of words encased forever in books."

Not only did I remember her, but her message brought to mind so many others who had made a strong connection to one book or another: a bright, but defiant, non-reader who after offerings and refusals of many books, finally latched on to *Breakfast of Champions* and went on to read all of Kurt Vonnegut's books. Bruce would be sprawled out in a bean bag chair, reading away, then suddenly burst into laughter, which also drew others to Vonnegut. There was the girl who was finally able to talk about a molestation after reading a novel that included the sexual molestation of a twelve-year-old girl, and the boy who read every YA novel I could find that featured an alcoholic father.

Candice's recent message conjured all of these and more, and I wondered as I was putting what I thought were the finishing touches on *Over 80* . . . why had I not included anything about books and reading?—such a big part of my life, of who I am.

I've always loved books, from my earliest memories of *Jack and the Beanstalk* and *Puss in Boots* and the Bible stories with the pretty illustrations, to the recently read *This is Happiness* and *The History of Rain,* both by Niall Williams. What a treat it is, at 86, to discover a new favorite writer. And what a thrill it was when I first learned to make sense of the written word.

My earliest experience with school left me disappointed and disillusioned. The instant I returned home from my first day in kindergarten, I ran into the kitchen, picked up the *Los Angeles Times* from the breakfast table, scanned the funny paper, and began to wail.

"What in the world is the matter with you, Marilyn?" my mother asked.

I could only cry.

"Did the children pick on you at school?"

I shook my head no.

"Was the teacher cross with you?"

Another negative nod.

"What then?"

"I can't read," I sobbed.

"Don't be silly. Of course you can't read yet."

"But Daddy told me when I went to school I would learn to read. And I went to school, and I still can't even read the funny paper!"

When my father came home from his meat market that evening, he opened a cold bottle of Budweiser and poured some into a glass that had once contained pink pimento cheese. He sat the bottle in front of his place at the table, and the little glass in front of my place. But instead of joining him right away, as was my custom, I sat under the high-ovened stove, next to Brownie.

"Come on up here, Shug, and tell me about school."

I sat, looking at bits of sawdust stuck to a glob of grease on the sole of his shoe.

"Don't you want your beer?"

"You lied to me," I said. "You tell me not to lie, but *you* lied to me."

His eyes flashed red as he grabbed me from under the oven and plunked me down in my chair in one swift move. He was a man who prided himself on his honesty, and did not take kindly to being called a liar by his five-year-old daughter.

"I can't read the newspaper," I told him, beginning to cry again. I reminded him of his promise that I would learn to read when I went to school.

"Didn't they teach you anything today?" he asked incredulously.

"We played with big blocks and sang," I told him.

He shook his head. "What kind of school is that anyway, Esther?" he asked, looking in the direction of my mother who was peeling potatoes at the sink. She did not respond to his question.

Again my father shook his head. Then he picked up his Budweiser and walked into the living room.

"I'll teach you to read," he said, reaching for a thin black book of Edgar A. Guest poems. I grabbed my beer glass and followed him.

We started with a poem called "Best Way to Read a Book" and my father explained that letters stood for sounds. He read a few words and then helped me puzzle one out and we went on that way, reading and drinking beer, until it was time for dinner. Now, upon rereading the poem, I see that it is sing-song-y and trite and sexist. But then, it suited me just fine, and I felt better about playing at school, knowing that I was learning to read at home.

A few months later the PTA sent out a bulletin on the pitfalls of parents attempting to help children learn to read. Different methods could lead to confusion, parents did not have special training, etc., but it was too late then. I had begun to make sense of the printed word, and no one could stop me. From the names of the Dionne quintuplets pictured in the bottom of my cereal bowl, to the signs for Morrell ham and Kraft cheese on the walls of my father's market, to the Buster Brown insignia inside my shoes, every understood word was a mystery unraveled and a sign of my own emancipation. Soon, I could read the funny paper for myself and not have to wait for one of my parents to get around to it.

From that first independent reading of the funnies to this day, reading has been a joy and a liberation. Books entertained, enlightened, comforted, educated, fed my soul, and they still do.

I was an excellent student through the sixth grade but that all changed in Junior High School and High School when I was expected to turn in homework and read books assigned by teachers. No way! Homework was an infringement on my outside time. And why would I read some boring assigned book when there so many other interesting books deserving of my attention?

Later, at twenty-six, divorced with two toddler girls, my job skills only qualified me for "Gal Friday" jobs that generally paid minimum wage of $1.15 an hour. Hardly enough to support a family of three. Having two young children totally dependent on me was the past due wake-up call that pushed me toward college with the intention of becoming a teacher. An awareness of such a later intention would have knocked my seventeen-year-old feet out from under me. But: decent pay. Benefits. A school schedule that would at least be partially compatible with my kids once they were beyond kindergarten. Hardly noble motivations, but necessary considerations.

Not having been a good student since the sixth grade, I worried that I was totally unprepared for college and that I'd not be able to do the work. But during those six years of not doing homework or reading assigned "literature," and the years that followed, I read *Fahrenheit 451, Exodus, Gone With the Wind, The Grapes of Wrath, Cannery Row*, everything by Frank Yerby, *Brave New World, On the Beach, God's Little Acre, Hiroshima*, everything by Mickey Spillane, *The Amboy Dukes, Lolita*, etc. I mostly read crap with a few more highly regarded titles tossed in. As academically unprepared as I was when I entered Pasadena City College in 1962, reading for pleasure had equipped me with a vocabulary, a sense of how a story went together, "reading stamina," and an intuitive understanding of plot and character.

At the end of my first year at PCC I received two small scholarships. The money didn't make a significant difference to me, but the votes of confidence from faculty gave me a huge boost. I was once again an excellent student. I was on the Dean's list all three of my years at Cal State L.A. (now California State University Los Angeles). So yes, thanks to reading books ranging from literary fiction to pap and drivel, I could do the work. Beyond that, through the power of reading, I broadened my scope and gained empathy for others, including those of different backgrounds and races.

In 1967, having gained my B.A. in English and a "California Standard Teaching Credential with a Specialization in Secondary Teaching," I began teaching English at Glen A. Wilson High School, a new school in a nearby fast-growing community. My schedule consisted of one Freshman and two regular Sophomore classes and one Advanced Placement Sophomore class. As I expect is a common experience for new teachers, after my first few weeks of daily preparations and late night paper grading, plus staff meetings and parent conferences and . . . and . . . and . . . I thought: WHAT HAVE I DONE??? But I gradually got better at managing the work. I enjoyed the students and my classes were generally fun and productive.

With my first paycheck (somewhere around $750 for the month), I took Sharon, eight, and Cindi, six, to their first-ever dental appointment, then sweetened the pot with new school clothes and shoes for them both. With the next paycheck it was my turn for catch-up dental work. Luckily, we all had good strong teeth and there was not much to be done even after years of absence from the dental chair.

Within the next several months we got a TV so the girls could watch Shirley Temple on Saturdays. Cindi got her first new two-wheeler and Sharon was able to start long wished-for piano lessons. Sharon took well to the piano lessons and we both took to the teacher, Mr. Reynolds. "We," the four of us, married in the summer of 1967. We became a family of five with baby Matt's birth in January, 1969, and for the next three years I was a stay-at-home mom. During that time I taught in night school programs while Mike and the girls watched Matt.

By Fall of 1972 when I was ready to resume teaching high school English, the only position available to me was at Century High School, the Continuation high school in the same district where Mike taught music. California Continuation high schools serve students who, for a myriad of reasons, can no longer attend their district's traditional high school. The student body at Century High School included some who were excluded from their home school because of gang-related activities, or drugs, or defiance of a teacher. Some just flat out hated school and were such poor attendees that they couldn't function in any of their classes.

Some undoubtedly had learning disabilities of one kind or another and a significant number came from difficult home circumstances. This was a much different demographic than the highly motivated, college-bound students in my previous teaching position and I expected to move to a "regular" high school when the next opportunity arose. Instead, I stayed at Century for twenty-six years. It turns out that my earlier experiences of blowing off school from the 7th through 12th grades enabled me to find common ground with my "underperforming" students.

The enrollment at CHS generally hovered somewhere around 180. Each year, out of those 180, there would be somewhere between twelve and twenty students who had found the support and encouragement they needed to make up credit deficits, complete requirements, and graduate. Often they were the first in their family to graduate from high school. Theirs were the success stories. But there were all of those others who'd attend CHS for a few weeks or months, and then leave their mom's house to live with their dad, or the family would go back to Mexico, or they'd get sent to juvenile hall, or kicked out of their house, or have to stay home to care for a younger brother or sister... or... or... If I could give such a kid a reading habit, it would be the gift of a lifetime. They could take the power of reading with them wherever they went.

For the next twenty-six years, my mission was to give every "I hate to read" student a love of reading before they left the realm of my influence. I stashed the district's required English curriculum binder in a corner closet, along with a class set of the 700-plus page *Adventures in Reading,* grammar textbooks, thirty-plus tattered copies of "Julius Caesar," and another twenty or so copies of *Great Expectations.* I love *Great Expectations*, but I wasn't ready to read it in high school. *Adventures in Reading* included plenty of good material but it was too much of a textbook to appeal to the "I hate to read" bunch.

I developed a classroom library of mostly paperbacks to fit a wide range of interests, and I made sure to include books that were frequently challenged, threatened with being banned. Challenged and banned books are often most interesting, and knowing a group of people want to keep a book from being read can pique the interests of reluctant readers.

With the help of a petty cash fund and a local bookstore, I fulfilled my students' book requests within a day or two. Silent reading time became the backbone of my program. Encouraging and developing a reading habit in my reluctant readers was the task to which I devoted most of my teaching energies. It was a task in which I believed wholeheartedly, except . . . there were those district level department meetings with *real* English teachers from *real* high schools. They couldn't possibly offer independent reading time at the expense of "Julius Caesar." And the ninth-grade teachers! They didn't have time to do *anything* but grammar! That was where the foundation was laid for all future writing. Their students would never learn comma usage if they didn't know their appositives!

Although I considered myself to be a good writer, I had not yet had anything published, and I lacked the courage to stand before my peers and confess that I couldn't tell an appositive from an appetizer, yet my comma usage was consistently error-free.

I would leave a meeting of district English teachers feeling that perhaps I was doing my students an injustice by not pounding in grammar and the classics. Maybe I was lazy because I wasn't turning myself inside out putting on highly motivating one-woman dramatic productions of "Julius Caesar." Was I simply self-indulgent because I spent part of my classroom time reading for my own pleasure?

As convinced as I was of the overriding importance of leading students to a reading habit, I lacked the confidence needed to spread the word to my English teacher colleagues because I lacked the basics of theory and research to support my intuitive approach to teaching.

Finally, I had the opportunity and good sense to pursue a master's degree. In 1981, I received an M.S. in Reading Education from Pepperdine University. The work I did during the course of that degree was challenging both academically and professionally, forcing me to evaluate my own teaching practices in the larger context of a cohesive teaching/learning theory.

My practice during that first decade at CHS had been simply to require that each day students read something that held meaning for them, and write something of meaning in their daily journals. Yes, we occasionally watched a movie. We frequently engaged in a degree of spontaneous group discussion. There was the occasional "beat the teacher" Scrabble game. Generally though, it was "read something *you* choose, and write something that comes from your heart."

The Pepperdine work helped me evaluate and modify what was effective and what was left wanting in my fly-by-the-seat-of-the-pants methods, and it also—both on a district level, and in my own personal reflections—added credibility to my classroom practices. It added significantly to my repertoire of techniques to help low-level readers, and I continued to direct my teaching energies toward guiding students toward books and activities that would be meaningful to them.

I shared my methods in workshops at education conferences and also in a book for teachers, *I Won't Read and You Can't Make Me: Reaching Reluctant Readers*. It's so very simple: Give students books that match their interests. Give them time to read. Be available.

Several years ago, the *Los Angeles Times* reported on a research study that showed the single most significant factor in determining a person's success in life was whether or not they read for pleasure. *That* they read was important; *what* they read was not. The study's definition of success included not only the obvious (in work and career), but also success in family and interpersonal relations, and in an enhanced sense of satisfaction with life in general.

The transfer from classroom experiences to real life is often not apparent. Yet isn't that why we work so hard to educate our youth? To better prepare them for life? What better preparation can we offer than a "reading for life" classroom, where student activities mimic those of adults who read for pleasure?

Except for the rare avid reader who entered my realm, complete with an interest in certain classics, or medical thrillers, or spy novels, or sci-fi, students entered CHS convinced that reading was boring and stupid. We desperately needed hundreds more books with which our at-risk students could connect.

From time to time a student would read one of those tattered "Julius Caesar" paperbacks. Occasionally I'd get a kid who was steeped in the "Lord of the Rings" series. The *Guinness Book of World Records*. Stories of disasters and survival. Books about cars and animals, especially those with pictures, garnered some interest. Mostly, though, students who browsed my bookshelves, or asked for recommendations, wanted to see aspects of life as they knew it reflected back to them.

With the continued emphasis on reading something of one's own choosing, my ongoing frustration was often in finding the right book for the right student. A significant number of students could get caught by *The Outsiders*, and *Go Ask Alice*. Books by Judy Blume often appealed to the "non-motivated" girls.

L.A. county juvenile hall must have had hundreds of copies of *Down These Mean Streets*, and

The Cross and the Switchblade, because boys newly released from "juvie," where they'd started but not finished such a book, often requested these titles. But after the limited tried and true choices—then what?

I followed Young Adult authors of the time who dealt honestly with difficult situations: Judy Blume, Chris Crutcher, Gloria Miklowitz, Gary Paulsen, Nancy Garden. I perused the American Library Association Best Books for Teens lists, and made trip after trip to the bookstore, often taking two or three kids with me. The Room 6 classroom library contained a wide variety of well-written, edgy books that indeed presented lives and situations with which many CHS readers could connect. Even so, in my first decade at Century High School, I couldn't find any realistic, non-preachy teen pregnancy or parenting stories—something a teen mom, or dad, could relate to. I found no teen fiction that might offer insight for one who had been sexually abused, nothing that reflected issues facing a teen in an abusive relationship.

Accepted statistics in the '80s generally stated that one out of three girls, and one out of six boys, would have had an unwanted sexual experience with an adult by the time they reached eighteen. Recent statistics from the National Center for Victims of Crime claim one in five girls, and one in twenty boys, is a victim of child sexual abuse. Such statistics are, of course, impossible to prove, but clearly the incidence of sexual abuse of children and youth is shockingly prevalent.

More out of desperation than ambition, I decided to try my hand at writing a story to fill the missing sexual abuse gap in my book collection. That decision led to the 1989 publication of *Telling,* my first teen novel. It is the story of a twelve-year-old girl who is molested by a neighbor. It took nine months to write. Two years—and twenty-two rejections later—it was finally published.

I'm sure I would have given up after the first ten or so rejections if it had not been for my student readers. I had a copy of my three-inch thick unpublished manuscript in a green three-hole binder, sitting on the classroom table. Slowly, unbelievingly, I noticed that several students were making it a point to get to class early to read it. I spent a significant portion of my next paycheck at Kinko's, making five more copies for classroom use, bought another $120.00 worth of postage stamps, and kept sending it out.

Another vacancy on my bookshelves needing to be filled was a realistic teen pregnancy novel. *Detour for Emmy* was my next book, and I found that the second book was much easier to get published than the first. After Emmy's story, I took on *Too Soon for Jeff,* teen pregnancy from a boy's viewpoint. I wrote two and a half books while teaching full time, but the necessary juggling act was not an easy one. If my husband and I went to a movie on the weekend, I felt guilty because it meant I wouldn't complete Chapter Four as planned. And if I skipped the movie and completed Chapter Four, I was guilt-plagued because my husband was getting short shrift.

Halfway through writing *Too Soon for Jeff* (this time with a contract and an advance), I decided to take to heart another adage from *The Artist's Way*, "Leap, and the net will appear." I'm nothing if not practical, and this is not an adage that I keep in mind when walking across bridges or standing near fourteenth-floor windows, but it was a very useful metaphor as I struggled with the "could I? should I?" early retirement decision.

I took one of those deals in which I would continue to teach twenty-five days out of the school year for a period of five years. This would supplement my meager retirement allowance, and, since I was writing realistic teen fiction, it would keep me in touch with my reading audience. From being a teacher/writer I became a writer/teacher and set about finishing book number three.

During that first writing year, somewhere in the middle of rewriting a paragraph, I sat at my computer in my home office, gazing out the window at squirrels stealing bird food, and laughing at our dog frantically jumping to reach the never-reachable squirrel, and contemplated my new life. I realized that even though I'd never been the sort of teacher you would ever see on TV proudly

holding high a "Best Teacher of the Year" trophy,
I had touched lives. I had been part of some amazing "turn-around" stories. And, as much as I rev-
eled in time to write, I missed the daily contact
with the wildly varied assortment of last-chan-
cers, and the thrill of their "this is the first book I
ever read" experiences. I wondered what I was
doing with my life. But then the letters, and later,
emails, came my way, and I realized my work was
still touching young lives.

*Hello Marilyn Reynolds! I have read all of your
novels . . . These books helped me realize that I don't
want to be a fourteen year-old mother. Right now I
just want to take care of myself and finish school.
Thank you.* Betty P.

I just finished reading But What About Me?
*and it was the most touching book I ever read. I'm a
guy but I can feel for her. Thank you.* S.V.

*I really enjoy reading your books . . . They have
helped me grow and be strong. And I know I'm not
alone in the world . . .* Caila M.

*Your books have turned non-readers into insa-
tiable readers as well as having opened up areas for
sensitive discussion. Your books have made life
"okay" for some of my girls who have discovered
their own personal situations in the books they are
reading. You need to know how much I/we appreciate your work . . .* Sandi Moon, teacher

Even though at this stage of my life, I'm no
longer directly engaged in the business of turning
disaffected youth into readers, it's reassuring to

know that my books continue to offer young readers perspectives on their own experiences, and to develop and increase their love of reading. Given the mess our nation is in today, it seems more important than ever that we have reading/thinking communities. I'm still a great believer in the power of reading.

The Gift of Reading— Part 2: The Little Free Library

I live in a quiet neighborhood at the corner of two streets that get a lot of foot traffic: people walking their dogs, or pushing a toddler in a stroller, or walking along while on a phone call or listening to a podcast, some speed-walking, some jogging. Within two blocks there are twelve to fifteen kids between the ages of five and eleven, kids who are often zipping around on their scooters or skateboards, riding bikes, or swinging from a saucer swing in one of their front yards. It's a perfect spot for a Little Free Library and I began trying to figure out how to get one. It should have two shelves, one low enough for the many younger kids in the neighborhood to browse and take books, and an upper shelf with room for a good selection of books for grown-up readers. The Little Free Library website showed just such a model but (yikes!) $389. Plus $150 for the post. The kits are a little less expensive but I have zero construction skills and the price would still be prohibitive. I tucked the Little Free Library idea into my lower subconscious near where I keep travel hopes, took myself to a nearby cafe where I had a too-large slice of chocolate cake and a cup of coffee doused with heavy whipping cream.

The Little Free Library idea lay dormant until one morning while driving home from the market I noticed a toddler's large red riding toy sitting at the edge of the curb, a large FREE sign on it. It had a bench where the kid could sit and grip the steering wheel while moving the "car" forward with his/her feet. I stopped, then backed up to get a better look. Hmmm. There was probably room for ten or so books in the back trunk. Another ten could go on the seat. I pulled what I later identified to be a Little Tykes Cozy Coupe to the back of my car, opened the trunk, and slid it in.

At home I gathered a batch of kids' books from assorted shelves in the house and boxes in the garage and fit them on the bench and in the trunk of the Coupe. I duct-taped a shallow empty box to the roof, and gathered an assortment of books I was unlikely to ever read again, stacked them in the box and labeled the box "GROWN-UPS." I turned a box lid into a sign:

FAIR WEATHER
OCCASIONAL
EXPERIMENTAL
LITTLE
FREE
LIBRARY

Shortly after I wheeled the Little Tykes Library to the edge of my sidewalk I caught sight of two of the neighborhood boys, probably around five and seven, shuffling through the books in the trunk. In the evening when I checked the "library" after wheeling it back into the garage, I saw that the kids' books were a jumble, with at least three of them "checked out." A couple of the adult books had also been "borrowed." To say I was thrilled would be an exaggeration, but I was pretty happy.

For years during non-school hours whenever I glanced out the corner windows just beyond my desk, some neighborhood activity would catch my eye. And now, with Covid and online schooling, off and on from sometime around ten in the morning until dark, the kids are out and about— on scooters and bicycles, fake sword fighting with cardboard shields, occasional tree climbing, and who knows what else? These days, though, browsing the car's books has been added to their activities. One of my favorite memories is of four-year-old Luke, barefoot and shirtless, his scooter cast aside at the curb, lying on his belly on the sidewalk, looking through a dragon picture book.

One evening, on my way out the door to put the LFL back in that garage for the night, I saw a giant red construction paper heart attached to the back of the car. "Thank You" was scrawled across the middle in uneven letters. Two names, in smaller, similar letters, were printed along the edge. There was also a childlike picture of a face beside the "u" in "Thank You." I brought the heart inside, printed "You're Welcome!" on the back, and reattached it where I'd found it.

I soon learned that middle-grade mysteries and dragon picture books were favored on the lower shelves. On the top shelf was historical fiction, James Patterson, memoir, literary fiction, and other books that defied categorization. New titles showed up fairly often, and books were often borrowed. It was always interesting to me as I secured the car library in the garage each night to notice what was new and what had been taken during the day. Not that I kept a running log, but some things were easy to notice, say the appearance of a thick copy of *Exodus* or a giant illustrated book on snails.

With the belief, or at least the hope, that every little bit counts, I began stripping my shelves of books by Black authors, fiction, memoir, and books that dealt directly with racism. *I Know Why the Caged Bird Sings, The Color Purple, Just Mercy, Caste, The Fire Next Time, The Hate U Give, The Warmth of Other Suns,* etc. A few of these went into the mobile library. The rest I spread around to other LFLs. I also occasionally added one of my own books from a surplus supply—a few copies of *Over 70 and I Don't Mean MPH, Love Rules,* and *Telling.* A friend who sometimes reviewed soon-to-be-released books donated ARCs (Advance Reading Copies).

Neighbors and other walkers would sometimes pause to chat about the LFL or books they'd enjoyed or donated. Occasionally a kid would ask if I had any more books about bugs, or Babysitter

Club books. Although the set up was less than perfect—I lost a few books the night I forgot to wheel the library back into the garage and the sprinklers came on; the adult books box kept needing to be re-taped and repaired—the Little Tyke Coupe served its purpose pretty well. It provided a range of books for would-be readers. There was no way to quantify whether or not the neighborhood kids were reading more, but they certainly were paying attention to the car books and often borrowing some. They and their parents were also often adding to the supply. And to some degree the LFL contributed to an increased sense of neighborhood community. It elicited smiles from earnest walkers, and sometimes book conversations between previously unknown neighbors. Plus, it was fun and always a treat to see kids interested in books.

One morning in church, about halfway through the sermon, Anara, who had not planned to attend that day, slipped in beside me and dropped my wallet into the straw purse I had sitting on the floor.

"I tried to call," she whispered. "I've been texting. This was in the Little Free Library. Talk later," she said, and quietly left the sanctuary.

At the final "Blessed be. Namaste. Amen," I rushed to my car, retrieved my phone, listened to the messages and read the texts. Neighborhood kids, three siblings ages eleven, eight, and four, had found my wallet in the LFL and taken it home to their mother, who became concerned. Had someone robbed me and tossed the wallet into the LFL? That made no sense because everything of value was still in my wallet: credit cards, I.D.s, about $60 in cash. Still it was concerning.

Although the mom and I chatted fairly often and had a few times shared drinks at outdoor gatherings, we'd never exchanged contact information. She did, though, have Anara's cell phone number. Anara knew I'd planned to go to church. My car was not in the driveway. That didn't explain why the wallet had been in the LFL, but it indicated that I was probably okay. When they couldn't reach me, Anara came to check things out personally.

Retracing my morning steps, I remembered I had, as usual, been running late. With my straw bag draped over my shoulder, I had rushed the LFL from the garage to its place at the edge of the sidewalk, then took a moment to fish around in my bag for my car keys. When I couldn't immediately put my hands on them, I pulled out a few items, including my wallet, and rested them on top of the kids' books. I found my keys, put stuff back in my purse, but apparently left my wallet behind.

I called Anara to thank her. She had reported back to the mom that I was indeed in church. They were both relieved that I was okay. It was troublesome to me, though, that I'd so carelessly left my wallet in with the books.

According to the experts, some memory loss is a normal part of aging. In his poem "Forgetfulness," Billy Collins talks of lost names, book titles, etc., "as if, one by one, the memories you used to harbor/decided to retire to the southern hemisphere of the brain/to a little fishing village where there are no phones." Sadly, in addition to being part of the normal aging process, memory loss can be an early sign of approaching dementia—perhaps the single biggest fear for me and my cohorts.

As disconcerting as my wallet glitch was, though, in keeping with my intention to not worry about the same thing more than three times in a day, I got on with my afternoon. After grabbing a quick bite to eat, accompanied by summer's ever-present iced tea, I wrote separate thank you notes to Luke, Walker, and Athena, the saviors of my wallet. I explained how difficult and costly it would have been for me to replace all that was in the wallet, and I included a $5 bill in each of their envelopes. (Was it $5, or was it only $2 or $3 each? I hope that it was five, but that memory also now resides in the southern hemisphere.) Only their dad was home when I delivered the notes but I later learned that the kids were thrilled with their rewards.

The next time I saw their mom I thanked her for raising such good kids. She gave a sort of ironic smile and allowed as how there had been some disagreement over whether to take the money before handing over the wallet.

"But they ended up doing the right thing," I said.

"They did," she said, this time with a full smile.

~

I wheeled the FAIR WEATHER (OCCASIONAL) EXPERIMENTAL LITTLE **FREE** LIBRARY out front in the morning and back into the garage in the evening every day from September 1, to October 22, 2020. Then, one afternoon, turning into my driveway, I saw nothing but grass where it had been just an hour or so earlier. I looked again. Had I already wheeled it back and forgotten? Not impossible, but no, it was not in the garage.

I stood looking dumbly at the blank space. I went back to my car, unloaded and put away the groceries, then walked back outside, as if staring again at the unoccupied space would yield some clues. One of the older neighborhood boys was across the street practicing some skateboard move.

"Hey, Walker, do you know what happened to the car library?"

To his credit, he didn't roll his eyes but picked up his skateboard and came across the street. Maybe he's still a year or two away from eye-rolling.

"I wondered where it was," he said.

"You didn't see anything?"

He shook his head, but soon we were joined by the trio of wallet-returners and another neighborhood girl, about five, I think.

"Do any of you know what happened to the library car?" I asked.

There was a flood of information. A garden lady took it. It was a red truck. Drove up and parked right across the street (this information accompanied by much pointing). She wheeled it across the street and put it in the back of her truck. The red truck? It was blue. No, it was red. I thought maybe she was doing it for you. Nope. Do you know who she was? No, just a garden lady. How did they know she was a garden lady? The other stuff that was in the back of her truck. Was anyone with her? Another garden lady. The truck was blue. It was red! What did she look like? Kinda big. Like bigger than you. Kinda dark skin. But not a Black lady. Brown hair. She was wearing a hat. More of a cap. Do you know where she does her garden work? No.

We all stared at the blank spot for a couple of seconds, then the kids went on their way. Athena came back to repeat "It was a RED truck."

I posted pictures of the car library on NextDoor, asking if anyone had seen anything. Asking that they be on the lookout. Saying reports were that the car library was taken by a gardening lady in either a red or blue truck.

I didn't count but would guess that over the next two or three days there were somewhere between thirty and forty responses. Many said how much they liked the car library and how awful it was that anyone would take it. Some were outraged. Many offered help in replenishing supplies. Some offered ideas for other inexpensive Little Free Libraries. And a few pointed out that my sign did include the word "Free."

Some days it seems that River Park is crawling with mow-and-blowers so I spent a few mornings driving around looking for a gardening lady with a red or blue truck. A neighbor said the people who came to the yard next to hers drove a red truck and sometimes a woman was there helping, but that turned out to be a false lead. In spite of my long ago hopes for following in Nancy Drew's footsteps, I turned out to be a poor excuse for a sleuth.

I know it's possible it was some greedy asshole that stole the car library, but I ultimately chose to believe the reason it was taken was the FREE sign. English is often a second language for many of the local yard people and "free" is likely to be more easily understood than "library." The car was taken in the middle of the day with others looking on, and it seemed a careful, unhurried process—no books were spilled out and left behind. Maybe the little car turned out to be a birthday present for a toddler. Maybe a few of the books got read, or the picture books well-thumbed.

Over lunch one Sunday, I told my Little Free Library tale of woe to Bob, a UU friend. Bob and I had both been caregivers for spouses with dementia and had written about our experiences. We became casual friends based on that commonality and we sometimes went to lunch together after church. After listening to me bemoan the loss of the LFL car and the cost of an official replacement, Bob said, "I'll build a Little Free Library for you."

Before retirement Bob's field was engineering and he liked building things. He had recently moved into a newly built eco-housing community and there were a lot of leftover materials and commonly owned tools which he was organizing. He said he'd like a project, plus the housing community also wanted a Little Free Library. Mine could be the prototype.

After clearing the project with my landlord, and with examples from the LFL website, modified to be sure that the lower shelf would be tall enough for picture books, Bob set to work. When he'd finished the basic construction, we set up a time for me to go out to his place and paint it. There was plenty of paint left over from the eco-housing construction so my LFL ended up with an eco-housing color scheme, a sort of tomato red with a yellow roof. It looks better than it sounds.

Once the painting was done, Bob and another UU friend came to my place with a post hole digger, sank a sturdy post into the hole, and secured it with concrete. A few days later they attached the LFL, being careful that all of the dimensions and angles were as they should be.

In spite of our care that picture books could fit on the lower shelf, it soon became obvious that it wasn't actually large enough to fully accommodate both adult and picture books. I solved that problem by using a rolling cart for kids' books. I was once again wheeling books out front in the morning and putting them back in the garage in the evening, though this time I chained the cart to the sturdy LFL post every morning.

A local artist brightened it all by painting ivy climbing up the post and around the edges of the roof. On the front of the peaked yellow roof sits an owl, reading a book. The decorating garnered a lot of attention from the kids who watched the whole process and offered plenty of advice. Although they never could agree on the color of the truck that made off with the car library, they did all agree that the owl should be named Star.

And so once again, I am the corner librarian. I don't see the personal evidence of a growing connection to reading as I once did in the classroom, but I trust that in my own small, random way, I'm still doing my bit for that life-changing process of reading, and of making the book connection. I recently heard the Stoics' motto on some podcast I was listening to as I walked the neighborhood. "Do what you can, with what you've got, where you are," or as a friend says, 'whatcha can, whenya can."

Grace & Gratitude for Life

A crisp November morning. Five of us, ages 60 to 85, are gathered on my front lawn, walking in place, being led by our exercise instructor to the beat of doo-wop music. Each of us stands to the right of a folding chair we've brought for the occasion. We've also brought weights, stretch bands, and mini-exercise balls.

Now it's double time, adding arms, reaching forward and then upward toward the sky. We pause for a quick stretch at the end of "At the Hop." I look up at the clear blue sky, filtered through a canopy of orange-tinged leaves, leaves that are loosening and will, within days, carpet the lawn.

I fill my lungs with fresh, clean air, appreciative that, at least for now, there are no fires burning California trees and structures. No smoke and dust particles of God-knows-what in the air. We do several rounds with weights, bicep curls, military presses, and something designed to tighten triceps but I don't think it's working, at least not for me.

Over the years my hand-weights have diminished from ten, to eight, to five, to three pounds. My eighty-five-year-old right shoulder balks at more than three. I could do most of the exercises on my left side with ten pounders, but I worry about becoming lopsided. *More* lopsided. I already list toward the right. I'm not sure what that's about. Maybe it's because of the habitual way I carry things, or a slight difference in leg length, or maybe it's to balance my left-leaning political stance. Whatever it is, I try not to make matters worse.

More stretches, more gazing skyward, more cleansing breaths of sweet fresh air. I am grateful for this day. This movement. Even grateful for the damned doo-wop music. There will come a time, sooner or later (though if I'm honest with myself that time will likely be on the side of sooner), a time when I will not be able to do this. To drag my chair and weights, exercise ball and stretch band from the garage to my front lawn, and double-time march, and stretch, and lift, and balance. I am aware of what a precious gift this is, this morning, this movement, this clean fresh air and loosening leaves, these trees, this lawn, these women gathered here, lighthearted, with a common purpose.

I remember my friend Greta, now long dead, whose exercise stopped suddenly back in the days of Jack LaLanne. And I consider my cousin, who is connected to oxygen because she can no longer take deep breaths of clean, fresh outdoor air. I thank Mimi Avocada for the great gift that has been given me through no special effort on my part, a gift that can only be attributed to grace, not the grace of my lopsided body but the mysterious, random grace of the universe, for which I am grateful beyond measure.

Down in Infamy

When I was very young, five or so, I would sit on a high stool at a tall metal bathtub while Mama Okura washed vegetables and talked to me in a strange sing-song voice. Usually it was enough just to listen and watch her fast hands swishing the carrots and potatoes around under the water, tossing them onto a wooden counter and reaching for more dirty vegetables from big gunnysacks at her feet. One time though, I thought she wanted me to say something in response. She seemed to be trying to tell me something important. I thought it was about a bridge, or water, and I pretended to understand because I wanted to go back to the old way where she talked and washed and I watched and listened.

Mama and Papa Okura owned the produce section in the southern California store where my father had his meat market. There were six boys in the Okura family, ranging in age from around fifteen to twenty-six. I could always understand the boys, but I could never understand what Papa Okura was saying. In fact, he hardly ever said anything to me. He did give me string beans to chew on, just as the rest of his family always did. I liked to watch him hose down and then sweep the cement floor at the front of the market, and I liked to watch him polish apples. His hands moved even faster than Mama Okura's did.

I especially liked the boys, and of them, I liked Ray the best. He would pick me up, ask a question, and then laugh. I liked how his eyes almost closed tight when he laughed.

Usually my parents referred to Mr. and Mrs. Okura as "Mama" and Papa" but sometimes it was "the Japs," as in "You can't beat those Japs for hard work," or "Those Japs keep the prettiest produce sections in town," or other kinds of work-related compliments.

One Sunday I heard that "the Japs" had bombed Pearl Harbor. My mother was crying because her sister, my Aunt Hazel, lived near there. When my grandmother got to our house, she was crying too. There were a lot of telephone calls and neighbors dropping by and constant talk about bombs and Auntie Hazel.

That afternoon, we learned that Uncle Henry had been wounded at Hickam Field. People started talking about "those dirty Japs." I thought about the Okuras, and the big metal bathtub, but I was afraid to ask any questions that day because I'd never seen my mother or grandmother cry before. When Auntie Hazel came home, she cried a lot, too. Uncle Henry had died from his wounds. They had been married three months.

One day when my aunt stopped by the market, Ray Okura told her he was sorry. I don't think she spoke to him, but I'm not sure because I only remember his face that day. I'd never seen him cry before, either.

Even before my aunt got back from Hawaii, Papa Okura had been taken away. He was accused of being a spy. My parents didn't think that was true, but they said in times of war you could never be sure.

It was not very many days after I saw Ray crying that the produce bins were empty and covered with canvas, and the whole family was gone. When I asked my mother where they were, she said they'd gone to camp. Someone else, who didn't wash the vegetables in the big tub or give me string beans, was now in charge of the produce department. He was okay, but I liked the Okuras better.

My mother and her friend, Willie, and I went one day to visit the Okuras at camp. I wanted to take my bathing suit because I knew camp was a place to swim and have fun, but my mother said it wasn't that kind of camp.

We drove to Santa Anita Racetrack, not far from our home in Temple City. A lot of people, all Japanese, were in the giant racetrack parking lot, living in tents and sitting on blankets under makeshift awnings. They didn't seem to be having a good time at this camp.

I didn't get to see Ray and his brothers because they were all in something called "quarantine." We did, though, see Mama Okura. My mother and Willie talked with her for a while, and gave her a package before we left. She walked with us to the gate and cried when she said good-bye. I ran ahead to stop the Good Humor truck. I wanted an ice cream for her, too. But when I turned to ask her what kind she wanted, she was already slowly walking back to her tent. She didn't hear me call to her.

On the way home, I asked why the Okuras had left the market to live in the camp. Willie told me that they had to because of what "the Japs" had done at Pearl Harbor and Hickam Field. We had to protect ourselves from "bad Japs." It was hard for "good Japs," like Mama Okura and the boys. But we were at war now, and we had to be very careful and very strong.

In the late spring I planted a victory garden. I wanted string beans, but my mother told me they were too much trouble, so I planted carrots and radishes. I began saving tinfoil, and stamps to be turned into war bonds, and my father collected rendered fat at his market. All of these things were to help us win the war. I was sure we would beat "the Japs." I hardly ever thought about the Okuras, except sometimes when I passed the string bean bin at the market and wished that I could just reach out and take one without getting into trouble, and eat it right then, and know that it was clean. But I was growing up, and some things had already passed from my life forever.

Assembling the Potato Salad

At first, the menu at our Stinson Beach gathering to celebrate My Favorite Son-In-Law's 65th birthday is to be tacos. There will be eleven of the family in attendance, the first time we've seen each other as a group in over a year.

"What might I bring?" I ask Sharon.

She pauses. Stumped. Except for eating, I'm not known for any expertise in the food department.

"Ummmm, salsa?"

I sense her hesitance. She's thinking maybe I'll buy the cheap Safeway salsa instead of the made-fresh-hourly Whole Foods Salsa. Or, worse yet, what if I bring *bottled* salsa??

"Sure. I can bring salsa. What else?" I tell her.

"Tortilla chips??"

"Okay."

And then it's as if the light goes on and she's come up with the perfect contribution.

"Tequila!" she says. "Bring a big bottle of Tequila for margaritas."

"That works," I tell her.

Another pause. She is, I'm sure, unhappily anticipating Costco's lowest-priced tequila and I'm pretty sure they'll have a back-up bottle of something highly-rated, and highly-priced, just in case.

It's margaritas, for God's sake. I'd like to run a taste test of margaritas made with the $52 bottle and those with the $21.95 bottle and see just how highly evolved Sharon and MFSIL's taste buds have become, but I suppose a 65th birthday celebration may not be the best time to try to prove a point.

We talk a bit more. "Any ideas on what to get the man who has everything? The one who buys things before he even knows he wants them?"

"I have no idea," she tells me. "The girls and I have bought him a blow-up paddle board for Stinson. I don't think he's ordered one for himself yet."

We laugh about MFSIL's buying habits. I'm generally judgmental about people who are so indulgent, so desirous of every new thing that comes along. Greedy consumers who accumulate more than they can possibly use when the world is full of starving people. Although I laugh about MFSIL's propensity for constant overbuying, he somehow escapes the harsher judgment I reserve for other over-consumers. For one thing, his family experiences no deprivation for the sake of his spending. For another, he is a generous soul, maybe slightly more generous with himself than with others, but ultimately generous all around.

Near the beginning of these reflections, I mentioned shuffling through a box of old photos in search for something that would embarrass or even amuse him. Nothing emerged that seemed worthy of the occasion. I'm afraid I have set the bar too high. On his fiftieth birthday I, with backup from Sharon, Marg, and Corry, serenaded him with an original composition, "I'm Doug's Mother-in-Law." Sung to the tune of "I'm My Own Grampa," it was funny, and smutty, and since I was unable to come up with anything comparable, I'll just have to rely on my capacity to spontaneously embarrass and mortify him. It's my duty as a mother-in-law!

Sharon and I catch up on other family news, affirm that I will indeed bring a big bottle of tequila along with chips and salsa, and sign off.

A week or so later, I get a text from Sharon saying they've decided on a more all-American 4th of July menu. She calls that evening.

"Fried chicken, biscuits, gravy, and corn on the cob," she says. "And Mom, could you, if it's not too much trouble . . ."

"Potato salad?" I say.

"That'd be great. Only if it's not too much trouble, though."

"It's not too much trouble," I tell her.

The tequila shifts to vodka for martinis and vodka tonics. Since we're on sort of a 1950's-themed fried chicken menu, we'll have potato chips and onion dip instead of tortilla chips and salsa. Sharon will take care of the chips and dip since I'm making the famous potato salad.

"You're sure it's not too much trouble?"

I again reassure her.

The potato salad is trouble, but I guess not too much trouble. It's probably the closest thing to a signature dish I have, though it's not really my recipe. It's my mother's, from her mother, and probably further back than that. They always referred to it as German potato salad, though they didn't claim German heritage. The years my grandmother was raising her family included WWI, and my mother's family-raising years included WWII, so it's a wonder they even admitted their potato salad was German. Regardless of its true heritage, the potato salad has become a family classic, and I'm the one who's left to make it, though Dale may make it after I've gone on to whatever is (or is not) next.

In the top drawer of my office file cabinet I find the folder "Esther's Memorial and Remembrances," and remove the handwritten recipe. Seeing my mother's handwriting pulls me away from today and back to a time that was *her* time— when she was fully in this world. Back when she wrote addresses on envelopes, absence excuses, and notes on Christmas cards. When she wrote numbers in ledgers, recording income and expenses for my father's business. When she enjoyed the horse races, playing pinochle, and perusing *Photoplay* magazine.

Although I know the recipe by heart, I'll keep her handwritten page out on the counter for security's sake. Who knows what memory tricks my eighty-five-year-old brain might play on me? It would be disastrous if I slipped and put celery in.

~

There was a time, before the war, when my mother made potato salad for sale in my father's market. She made it once a week, in a giant royal blue ceramic bowl from the J.A. Bauer factory where Milton, my Aunt Ruth's pedophile husband, worked. I never met Milton who was in jail by the time I was old enough to watch my mother fill the bowl with potato salad. She loved that bowl and it was one of her life's many great disappointments when, fifty-two years after making her last commercial potato salad, as she was moving things around in her kitchen, a big chunk broke off of the rim, and the bowl was of no more use.

When I was two, or maybe three, my nineteen-year-old cousin, Jim, came from Arkansas to live with us and to learn the meat business from my father. With his quick smile and easy laughter, it was love at first sight for me. Jim has been dead for over thirty years and I still hear his rolling laughter, feel my delight as he danced me around the living room singing "Chattanooga Choo Choo."

But this is about potato salad.

My mother always made the potato salad on Wednesday, which was Jim's day off. I remember watching the potato peels fly as I sat at the table in the yellow-tiled kitchen. I remember Jim juggling potatoes, rushing to peel them when they were still too hot to handle, my mother chopping onions and peeling the eggs while bacon cooked in the black iron skillet, all this at top speed, determined to get it thrown together and delivered to the market by 1:00, in time for them to make the second race at Santa Anita.

Having studied the newspaper picks the night before, and maybe the Racing Form, they bantered about who they liked, who was favored to win. "Aren't you tired of losing money on that horse?" Or, "You're betting him? He belongs behind a plow!" Laughter and hustle filled the little kitchen.

Of course I longed to go to the races with them. What kid wouldn't? But no matter how long, or how often I begged, on horse race days I was always dropped off at Granny's on their way to the track.

My mother always insisted that I was too young to go to the races.

"When will I be old enough?"

"Maybe when you're eight."

She might as well have said, "When you're thirty." Eight sounded that far away.

The first time I went to the racetrack, I was only seven, but the horses weren't running. Racing had been suspended and Santa Anita was being used as a temporary detention center for Japanese-Americans. I'd gone with my mother to visit the Okura family there. I wanted to see the boys, Benny and Ray, but they were in quarantine. Only their brother, Charlie, was sitting with his mother under an awning on a tarp in the parking lot. Papa Okura had been arrested, suspected of being a spy. My mother gave Mama Okura the blankets and soap she'd brought from home. The only other thing I remember from that first trip to Santa Anita was the high towers that lined a heavy chain link fence, and soldiers with guns standing in each tower looking out over the parking lot.

Later, after the Okuras and all the other imprisoned Japanese citizens were sent to more permanent facilities, Santa Anita served as a prisoner-of-war camp and an army training center. Because Jim and another butcher were drafted into the army at the beginning of the war, my mother traded her potato salad contributions to help my father behind the counter of his meat market. Jim was still in New Guinea when Santa Anita reopened.

~

I'm too slow in the kitchen. If I had to make ten pounds of potato salad on one of those Wednesdays, I never would have made the second race. This is what happens when I make my mother's, my grandmother's, my great-grandmother's potato salad. With the first cut of a warm potato, I am suspended between long ago and now. As I fry the bacon in my non-stick skillet, I smell it frying in the old cast-iron frying pan on the front burner of the O'Keefe and Merritt stoves. I'm drawn back to that kitchen, to Jim's free and raucous laughter, to my mother in her apron. I smell the sawdust in my father's market, hear the increasing rumble of the crowd as the horses approach the finish line.

Although it's meant to be served warm, I put together the potato salad the day before I'm to join the group at Stinson Beach. There will be enough kitchen activity without me complicating things with my potato salad project. Besides, I'd rather spend time on the deck overlooking the water than in the kitchen.

I assemble the ingredients in a four-quart pink Pyrex bowl, a bowl left over from my long-ago first marriage. It's a miniature bowl in comparison to my mother's old giant royal blue potato salad bowl, but it's large enough to contain sufficient servings to feed a crowd. For the sake of food safety, I leave out the Miracle Whip and take an unopened jar with me. Best to mix it in just before serving.

By three on the afternoon of the party the celebrants have arrived. Sharon and Doug's grown daughters are there with their partners. Dale and Marg, Corry and Amy, and a couple from Lake Tahoe who are longtime friends of Sharon and Doug's. Our Airbnb is on the lagoon side with a large deck overlooking the water. The day is sunny and comfortably warm. Two white clouds float overhead in contrast to the sapphire sky. Throughout the afternoon, in various configurations, there are kayaking, stand-up paddle boarding, corn hole competitions, individual book reading, conversations around the table on the deck, and general levity.

MFSIL and Subei's hefty boyfriend help lower me into a kayak that's tied to the dock. It is, I know, a humiliating sight. I'm glad Doug's hands are full with helping me, so he is unable to reach his phone and record the awkward maneuver.

Once in the kayak, the rope loosed from the dock, I paddle/glide with ease around the lagoon. The water is smooth and clear, the sun warming my SPF 50 protected face. Subei is standing on the paddle board, coming across the lagoon with a long paddle. When did that start? All my friends and I knew to do with a paddle board was to lay on our bellies and scoop water with our cupped hands. I'll keep that paddle board information to myself when I join the others back on the deck. We oldsters need to be careful not fall into too much "back in my day . . ." talk which soon deadens conversation.

Sometime before sunset, after a day of kayaking and paddle boarding, corn hole "tournaments" and lounging about, we all gather around a table on the deck to toast MFSIL. Sixty-five seems young to me now, but it didn't seem young back when I hit that marker and I know it doesn't seem young to Doug. He is fit, exercises regularly, eats well. He and Sharon are already following the Four Pillars of Healthy Aging: Exercise, Nutrition, Purpose and Connection. Still, they're not free of the inevitable decay that comes with time and gravity. Their descent into the young-old category is as unsettling to me as my own descent into the old-old category. How is it that my baby has deepening crow's feet, joint swelling and pain? How is it that her young groom is now totally gray and regularly in bed by 9:00? And how is it that my neck has grown turkey wattles and new age spots appear on my face and hands with the frequency of unwanted junk mail?

Never mind, this is about potato salad and a party. Amid gales of laughter we toast MFSIL with martinis and whatever other beverages people prefer. I don't remember now exactly what was so funny—much affectionate bantering I'm sure, maybe a bit of cynical laughter over the vagaries of the current political situation. Although I don't remember the specifics, I do remember the lightness of the mood, the shared affection, the joy at finally coming together after our seemingly interminable Covid-related separation.

In the evening, we gather inside at the long, food-laden table. There, among fried chicken, corn on the cob and biscuits, sits the pink bowl of potato salad. For the partners of each of Sharon and Doug's daughters, and for their Lake Tahoe friends, this is just some potato salad. For the rest of us, though, to varying degrees, the first bite carries history, and story, and family.

Later, having eaten our fill, and a bit more, we linger at the table, talking, not quite ready for the party to end. Corry asks, "Who do you think you'll pass the potato salad recipe on to for after you're gone, Auntie M?"

"It's there for the taking, in Granny's remembrance file," I tell her.

"Who do you think will make it?"

I shrug. "I don't know. Maybe Dale. Maybe Cindi. Maybe you, if you someday get a hankerin' for it. Or maybe no one."

We laugh. The truth is, the tradition of this particular potato salad may leave the world when I do. Or maybe Dale will then make it a few times and it will leave the world when he does. He and I probably like it better than anyone else. Most of it was eaten tonight and I know they like it, but others may be ready for a change. Maybe something with tofu bacon. And celery. No more crass Miracle Whip. It will be mixed instead with extra virgin olive oil from olives grown and harvested under humane conditions in the hills of Montepulciano.

Sometime after midnight, as I hover on the edge of sleep, I sense the potato salad spirits. Granny, Jim, my mother and father, the blue bowl, the yellow tiled kitchen, all sink back to their rightful place in my subconscious mind. There, they and countless others, will lie in wait until something, maybe a faint whiff of cigarettes and beer, a pot roast dinner, a long-forgotten tune, drags them back to the surface of my consciousness where they can stay for a while, but not too long.

I wonder, when the time comes that I only exist in the subconscious minds of the people I love, what is it that will bring me back for a short visit?

Sears Family German Potato Salad

5 LBS. POTATOES
1 DOZEN EGGS
2-3 MEDIUM BROWN ONIONS
1 LB. BACON
BACON GREASE
MIRACLE WHIP MAYONNAISE
DASH OF APPLE CIDER VINEGAR

Boil potatoes until tender. Dump in sink to cool.

Hard boil eggs. Dump in sink.

Chop onions.

Cut bacon crosswise into half-inch strips. Fry until crisp. Save bacon grease.

When potatoes cool enough to handle, peel and cut into bite sized pieces.

Peel and cube hard boiled eggs and add to potatoes. (Reserve one egg to grate on top when finished.)

Add bacon and mix ingredients.

Pour 1/4 cup or more bacon grease into mixture.

Add about 1/2 cup Miracle Whip, 1/4 cup vinegar, and sugar.

Add salt and pepper to taste. Mix well. Adjust dressing and seasonings.

Serve warm.

Note: Miracle Whip was not invented until 1933. My grandmother would have been fifty-two then, and would already have made an abundance of non-Miracle Whip potato salad. She, her mother, and those who came before them must have made their own mayonnaise/dressing for their potato salad. I don't know if it was my grandmother or my mother who modernized the recipe with the short-cut Miracle Whip, probably my mother.

ACKNOWLEDGMENTS

This book would have remained an unfinished file in my over-burdened laptop were it not for the support and expertise of so many. For their help I am forever grateful.

To Jan Haag and the Team Haag writers for appreciation of first draft snippets and for the reassurance that comes with laughing in the right places. Thank you for helping me see that the over 80 perspective was worth a book.

To the Monday afternoon writers, Victoria Hemingson, Karen Kasaba, and Deborah Lott. Thank you for constructive critiques, mutual support and shared commiserations. You kept me moving forward.

To Dave Dawson, Dale Dodson, Anara Guard, and Judy Laird for in-depth readings and shared insights, and for catching inconsistencies and questionable details, always with a kind spirit, and for your ever-present encouragement. I truly can't thank you enough.

Thanks also to New Wind Publishing's Dave Hutchinson and Anara Guard for their consistent good humor, view of the big picture, book production expertise, and so much more, and to Gay Guard-Chamberlin for her careful editing and for her capacity to ask the right questions.

To Dale and Marg Dodson, Sharon Reynolds-Kyle and Doug Kyle, Subei Reynolds-Kyle, Lena Reynolds-Kyle, Matthew Reynolds, Leesa Phaneuf Reynolds, Mika Reynolds, Cindi Foncannon, and Beth Silverstein. Thank you all for shared food, drink, and laughter, for conversation both light and not, and for your ongoing general support along this long and winding way.

Thanks to the broad community of Sacramento writers, to the UUSS community, and to the Callister/Minerva-Spilman/Sandburg River Park neighborhood. My life is enriched and enlivened by such connections.

ABOUT THE AUTHOR

Marilyn Reynolds is the author of numerous books including the memoir, *'Til Death and Dementia Do Us* Part, the story of her husband's losing battle with frontotemporal dementia. Her popular and award-winning realistic teen fiction series, True-to-Life from Hamilton High, consists of eleven titles. She has also written a book for educators, *I Won't Read and You Can't Make Me: Reaching Reluctant Teen Readers* and the collection of essays, *Over 70 and I Don't Mean MPH.* She has a variety of published personal essays to her credit and was nominated for an Emmy for the *Too Soon for Jeff* teleplay.

Ms. Reynolds worked with reluctant learners at a southern California alternative high school for more than two decades. She lives in Sacramento where she enjoys neighborhood walks, visits with friends and family, and the luxury of reading at odd hours of the day and night.

www.marilynreynolds.com

YOU MIGHT ALSO ENJOY THESE BOOKS
BY MARILYN REYNOLDS

Over 70 and I Don't Mean MPH: Reflections on the Gift of Longevity

Written in a conversational tone with honesty and humor, this essay collection offers a compelling look at experiences and situations common to people over 70. Part inspiration and part how-to, the writings explore subjects such as choosing a burial or cremation plan, living in a body that requires high maintenance, and being typecast as one who can only eat bland foods. The personal essays expose with irony and humor the often overlooked details of the trials of aging, yet also provide a deeper understanding of the necessity of reinvention late in life.

Til Death or Dementia Do Us Part

In her compassionately written memoir, Marilyn Reynolds provides a detailed account of her husband's puzzling symptoms of Frontotemporal Dementia and of his gradual decline. This book will be helpful to many who have loved ones suffering from dementias of all types. Marilyn takes readers on a journey from the very early signs of the disease, through the emotional and practical adjustments required, changes to financial and living arrangements, etc., as her husband's disease progressed. It is written honestly and directly, and with courage.

Order from your local bookseller or directly from
www.NewWindPublishing.com

CPSIA information can be obtained
at www.ICGtesting.com
Printed in the USA
BVHW051232041122
651158BV00004B/801